Tiffany Olson

REAL LEADER.
REAL LEGACY.

THE POWER OF LEADERSHIP AT EVERY STAGE OF YOUR WORKING LIFE

Copyright © 2025 by Tiffany Olson

All rights reserved. No part of this book may be reproduced or used in any manner without the written permission of the copyright owner, except for the use of quotations in a book review. For more information, contact olson_tiffany@msn.com.

ISBN Paperback: 979-8-9996895-0-4
ISBN Electronic: 979-8-9996895-1-1
Library of Congress Control Number: 2025920899

Publishing consultant, PRESStinely: PRESStinely.com

Portions of this book are works of nonfiction. Certain names and identifying characteristics have been changed.

First Edition
Printed in the United States of America

TIFFANY OLSON
Find additional resources, tools and inspiration at
TiffanyOlson.net

Connect with Tiffany on LinkedIn
LinkedIn.com/in/OlsonTiffany

Disclaimer

The stories and resources shared in these pages were designed to help you thrive in your working life. Of course, I can't guarantee your results. Your ultimate success relies on your own efforts. The personal stories I've shared reflect my present recollections of experiences over time. Some names have been omitted, some events have been compressed and some dialogue has been recreated. I've researched the stories about companies and supported them with footnotes. These sources are resources to support you in your journey. I wish you courage and resilience as you build your leadership legacy.

— Tiffany Olson

To Brad, Jess and Kevin.
This journey is for you.
You are my heart and the source of my strength.

Acknowledgments

This book would not exist without the encouragement, wisdom and generosity of so many people who walked alongside me on this journey.

To **Syd Atlas** — my coach, my steadfast believer and my inspiration. A distinguished author of three books, you've shared your wisdom and gifts generously with others — and with me. This book was born from your idea, and your unwavering belief made it possible. You reminded me to trust myself and keep going. Our video calls filled with encouragement meant more than I can ever express. Over the years of working together, we became friends — and that has been the greatest gift of all.

I feel deeply fortunate to have had the chance to work alongside so many remarkable people over the years and to learn from them. I'm especially grateful to the leaders I admire and had the opportunity to interview for this book — **Joe Capper, Derek Maezold, Cathy Langham, Ann Murtlow** and **Rod Cotton.** Thank you for trusting me with your stories. You shared your experiences, vulnerabilities and journeys of leadership with openness and honesty. Your candor brought depth, humanity and richness to these pages.

To **Tom Searcy**, an advisor, author and friend — thank you for asking the hard questions that pushed me to think deeper and write better. And to **Monique DeMaio,** for your thoughtful advice on navigating the process and creating something meaningful.

Real Leader. Real Legacy.

To the talented team who helped shape these words into something stronger: **Alyssa Chase**, writer, editor and perfectionist — your guidance and creativity made this book whole. With your long and distinguished career, you brought not only talent but also a depth of insight that elevated every page. I appreciate your belief in this work. **Nicole Keller**, whose careful eye as copy editor brought clarity to every page. And **Zora Knauf**, who offered thoughtful edits with grace while embracing the joys of new motherhood. Your skill and care transformed this manuscript, and I am deeply grateful.

Finally, to **Kristen Kasza-Wise** and **Maira Pedreira** of PRESStinely — thank you for bringing this book into the world with such care and commitment.

Most of all, thank you to my family and friends, who cheered me on at every milestone — from the first draft to the finished book. You celebrated each small victory with me, reassured me when I doubted myself and reminded me why I started. Your love, patience and unwavering support have made this journey possible.

— Tiffany Olson

Contents

Introduction 13

Chapter 1
Independence Builds Resilience; Kindness Builds Leaders 17
    Independence through idleness 18
    A family legacy of resilience 20
    Kindness goes a long way 21
    Kindness is a leadership skill … and a life skill 21
    Joe Capper: a case in kindness 23
    Kindness in crisis 23
    TIFFANY'S TAKEAWAYS 25

Chapter 2
Own Your Uniqueness so You Can Challenge the Status Quo 27
    "I don't want to play Barbie. I want to make a business plan!" 28
    Curiosity: the secret sauce to success 28
    Tesla: disrupting the automotive industry 29
    Challenging the status quo: asking questions 31
    Warby Parker: disruption through uniqueness 31
    TIFFANY'S TAKEAWAYS 34

Chapter 3
Implement Ownership Culture 37
    Not just a job 39
    Results = success 40
    Leading change without losing people 41
    Not just a beer 44
    TIFFANY'S TAKEAWAYS 45

Chapter 4
Embrace the Journey 47
    A growth mindset 48
    If at first you don't succeed: insights from global leaders 49
    When the journey gets rough… 51

My Janesville moment 52
TIFFANY'S TAKEAWAYS 55

Chapter 5
Put the Customer First, Not the Numbers 57
"Learn the customer and you'll learn the business." 58
Cases in excellent customer service 59
Managing versus leading 63
Putting the customer first 64
Centering the customer: a formula for lasting success 65
How to put the customer first 66
Relevance is key 67
TIFFANY'S TAKEAWAYS 68

Chapter 6
You Can't Succeed Alone 69
Asking for help 69
Courageous conversations 74
Ben & Jerry: a dynamic duo 75
Finding balance by leaning on others 78
Sometimes leadership isn't linear 81
Leaders help in small but important ways 82
Family first 83
Celebrate your contributions 84
TIFFANY'S TAKEAWAYS 86

Chapter 7
Take Risks (as a Team) 87
A risk can change everything 88
Netflix: revolution through risk 88
Spanx: Sara Blakely's big risk 90
Risk-taking: a team effort 92
TIFFANY'S TAKEAWAYS 94

Chapter 8
Prioritize What Matters Most 95
Our family command center 96
Lean practices: standup meetings and visual metrics 97
Boundary setting 100

The beauty of breaks and boundaries 101
Making work and family life work 103
Building relationships at work 104
TIFFANY'S TAKEAWAYS 105

Chapter 9
Overcome Imposter Syndrome and Share Your Authentic Story ... 107
Imposter syndrome: a silent struggle among high achievers 108
Power poses: bodies building confidence 109
Building confidence by embracing challenges 109
Bringing the walls down 111
Connecting across cultures 112
Storytelling as a leadership tool 112
"You couldn't make it up!" 113
Practice makes perfect 114
TIFFANY'S TAKEAWAYS 116

Chapter 10
Listen, Learn and Lead 119
A method that works in any workplace 119
LISTEN 122
LEGO listens 122
Safety in sharing, success in teamwork 123
LEARN 124
LEAD 125
Defining your vision 126
TIFFANY'S TAKEAWAYS 129

Chapter 11
Don't Be Afraid to Be Vulnerable 131
From providing to receiving: my story of raw vulnerability 131
Health equity and cancer: purpose through vulnerability 134
Stories of triumph: vulnerability to victory 138
Reckoning and rumbling with Brené Brown 140
TIFFANY'S TAKEAWAYS 143

Chapter 12
Pick the Right Strategy and Celebrate the Wins 145
Recovered and ready for my next role 145

Effective communication: a winning strategy ... 148
Choosing the right moment to act ... 149
Strategy successes and failures in big business ... 150
The wall of wins ... 152
Creating a culture of appreciation ... 154
TIFFANY'S TAKEAWAYS ... 155

Chapter 13
Find Your Next Career Chapter ... 157
Becoming a big-picture leader through board work ... 157
Considering joining a board? ... 159
Questions for evaluating board service ... 163
A legacy of continued leadership ... 164
The power of mentorship ... 164
TIFFANY'S TAKEAWAYS ... 167

Conclusion
Your Leadership Legacy ... 169

Featured Leaders ... 171
Joe Capper ... 171
Rod Cotton ... 172
Cathy Langham ... 174
Derek Maetzold ... 175
Ann Murtlow ... 177

About the Author ... 179

Author's Note

When I was born, my mom thought I looked like a jewel. That's why she named me Tiffany after the iconic jeweler Tiffany & Co.

Betty Jean "B.J." Norgaard's unwavering support and love filled me with self-confidence. We always talked about my life as if it were a precious stone we could facet and polish together, just like a Tiffany diamond.

My mom didn't finish college. She divorced when I was a young girl and worked throughout my childhood. Her example of living by her wits, along with her endless encouragement, cultivated my strength and independence before I even understood those qualities. She raised me with an elegant design in mind, pushing me to rely on myself — to complete my degree, earn my MBA, build a successful career and take calculated risks with confidence.

My mother's gift to me is my gift to you. That's why you'll see images of diamonds throughout this book. The diamonds are for you! Think of them as symbols of your own life's journey. I hope this book and its stories will help you to chisel and polish your career and build your leadership legacy.

Introduction

Leadership is a gift you can give and receive.

The backseat of my Audi A6 was piled with so many flowers, I felt like I was at my own funeral. The boxes were stacked so high, they blocked my rearview mirror. I could barely close the trunk. It's interesting what you take with you when you retire: the nameplate, of course; the photos of the team and some extra Post-its — because you never know when you might need more of those. As I drove out of the parking lot for the last time, I couldn't help but wonder, "Is this it? This is it. This is really it. Now what?"

One traffic light from home, I heard my phone buzzing. I glanced down and saw it was my friend Sally. I assumed she was calling to congratulate me on my retirement, but when I answered, I heard her voice trembling. She was crying, barely able to speak. I pulled over. Between gasping sobs, she told me someone else got the promotion that she had been promised. She felt disappointed and angry that she had been treated unfairly. She didn't know what to do next.

I sat in the car for the next hour, surrounded by the scent of lilacs and boxed-up mementos, talking her through her options. We discussed the next steps: talking to her boss, polishing her resume, reaching out to her network and staying resilient. I told her I believed in her and reminded her of what I saw in her. By the end of the call, Sally sounded like her usual, courageous self. She told me how much better she felt — how good it was to talk with someone experienced, someone rooting for her. As I pulled away from the curb and drove home, a realization hit me: This is my new path.

Most people think becoming a leader is about climbing the ladder — getting the next job, more responsibility, more people to manage. I used to believe that, too. But I'm here to tell you, real leadership is about legacy. It's about what you do when you've reached the top or, perhaps, when you step down and yet still have so much to give. It's about investing in others, not because you're obligated but because you know the importance of lifting others as you go.

This book is for anyone who's ever asked, "What's next?" Whether you're just starting out, hitting your stride or approaching a transition, this book can help you discover the power of leadership at every stage of your working life. You don't have to be a seasoned professional to make an impact. You don't need years of experience or a fancy title to lead. You can lead from where you are right now.

The chapters that follow outline the lessons I've learned as a leader. Each chapter includes not only my personal stories but also stories from leaders in global business and successful leaders I know personally. You can learn more about the leaders I know in the Featured Leaders section at the back of the book. In the pages that follow, I'll share true stories from this diverse group of leaders to inspire you in your personal leadership endeavors.

This book isn't just about learning; it's about taking action. The "Tiffany's Takeaways" at the end of each chapter are short, actionable tips you can quickly skim and apply to your life right now, both personally and professionally, no matter your profession.

Approach this book however you'd like. It's up to you and your particular learning style!

Whether you're starting out or winding down, whether you're at the top or still climbing, I invite you to take what you need from these pages. Leadership is a gift you can give — and receive — at any time, and it's a gift that keeps on giving. So take what you learn and pass it on to others.

CHAPTER 1

Independence Builds Resilience; Kindness Builds Leaders

In the face of adversity, resilient leaders inspire confidence in their teams.

Resilience and kindness may seem like two very different attributes, but it takes both qualities to lead effectively. They're two sides of the same coin.

Independence plays a crucial role in building resilience by empowering people to face challenges with confidence. When you learn to navigate difficulties on your own, often by making mistakes and learning from them, you develop resilience. Independence fosters grit and toughness. As your independence grows, you begin to trust your ability to overcome obstacles, even in the face of adversity. With each challenge, you'll cultivate more resilience, allowing you to bounce back faster and better from life's challenges.

Real leaders know that resilience is crucial because it empowers them to navigate setbacks and uncertainty with strength. In the face of adversity, resilient leaders remain focused, adaptable and optimistic, inspiring confidence in their teams and maintaining momentum toward goals. They're able to recover quickly from failures, learn from mistakes and model strength and perseverance to their teams. This not only builds trust, loyalty and respect among team members but also fosters a culture of resilience within the organization, empowering others to stay motivated and committed, even when times get tough.

But resilience isn't all you need for leadership. Often, toughness must be tempered with tenderness. Kindness doesn't equate to weakness, like many who implement old-school leadership approaches still believe. A compassionate approach won't compromise your authority. You can have empathy and make tough decisions.

Nice guys and gals don't finish last, especially in the leadership world. Leading with kindness strengthens relationships and creates a positive and inclusive environment where people feel valued and respected. A kind leader listens with empathy, communicates with compassion and supports others through both personal and professional challenges. This approach not only boosts morale and engagement but also encourages collaboration among team members. When leaders lead with kindness, they set a powerful example that cultivates a culture of trust and psychological safety — essential ingredients for long-term success.

Independence through idleness

At the age of 7, I could get up on my own, brush my teeth, make breakfast, get dressed and go to school. When I see how kids are being raised today, I want to shout, "Give them independence! Give them a place to roam on their own and find their own way! Give them a chance to make mistakes and get back up on their own!"

The fact of the matter is, "helicopter parents" are raising kids who will become your colleagues or maybe even your bosses and, if they've spent their entire lives being chauffeured from A to B, never having experienced an idle moment because there's always a smartphone with a cat video available, working together won't be easy. If you're a leader in your workplace, you'll need to find a way to foster a sense of independence and self-efficacy in these team members and the best way to do so is through your example.

Maybe you were raised by a helicopter parent and, if you were, the important thing now is that you recognize it and work to give yourself the independence that you didn't have as a child.

Why is this important? Esther Perel is a Belgian-American psychotherapist known for her work on human relationships. Besides her famous TED Talks about the complexities of love relationships today, she's an iconic couples' therapist. A few years ago, she started a podcast called "How's Work?" Her theory is that who you are outside of work naturally shapes your workplace connections, conflict and dynamics. If you haven't fully achieved independence outside of work, you're not going to react to challenges in the workplace with maturity and poise.[1]

It's all well and good to say we need to be more independent but, as adults, how do we actually cultivate this trait, especially if we, for all intents and purposes, are independent — living on our own and providing for ourselves?

We cultivate the spirit of independence through idleness, Perel says. It's not only kids who need space to be bored, but adults, too. Our smartphones often function as babysitters for our minds, keeping us occupied and giving us something to do when we feel restless. If you can relate to this, now might be the time to unplug or undergo a digital detox. By intentionally working to increase your level of independence, you'll cultivate resilience.

---

[1] Lewis Howes, "Greatness Clips: Autonomy VS Loyalty: Esther Perel," The School of Greatness, accessed August 12, 2025. YouTube, 38 sec., https://www.youtube.com/watch?v=PyOsBDYq2Ls.

A family legacy of resilience

I've worked in the C-suites of international Fortune 100 companies and served as president and CEO. I've led teams of over 4,000 with revenue over $1 billion, and I now serve on the boards of several innovative healthcare companies. But what I learned most about being a leader I learned from my mother, Betty Jean "B.J." Norgaard.

My parents divorced when I was around 8 years old and my father soon left town, so my older brother, Kilb, and I were raised by a single mom. Single motherhood is hard at any time, but in the 1960s, it was rare. All my friends' mothers were happy homemakers — or at least homemakers.

Although she'd been active at the University of Minnesota and helped found a sorority there, Mom married at age 23 and never completed her degree. A speech and theater major, she shared her love of music and dance with both me and my brother. Later, she did some modeling and became a speaker and acted in commercials.

Newly divorced at age 38, Mom embodied the quality of resilience. She took whatever job she could get — from cashier to delivery driver, advertising to sales. Sometimes she worked two jobs at once. She eventually held jobs at General Mills and as a residence manager for the 35th governor of Minnesota, Al Quie, and his wife, Gretchen.

Mom taught me that no job is beneath you, and every job deserves your best. She taught me the value of work and that working hard meant trying and not giving up.

The side effect of being raised by a single mother was that I not only learned to be independent and self-sufficient early on, but I also learned the importance of resilience.

At the beginning of my professional life, many of my leadership ideas came from my mother, who was a wizard at doing more with less. I watched Mom deal with a myriad of personalities and never lost her sense of worth — of who she was and what she was able to give the world. She embodied Oscar Wilde's philosophy: "Be yourself; everyone else is already taken."

Kindness goes a long way

There was another female role model who made a profound impact on my leadership style. On the first day of second grade at Neil Armstrong Elementary School in Golden Valley, Minnesota, I woke up late like I did every morning, got dressed and ran downstairs to make breakfast, which consisted of toast, peanut butter and cereal. I was in such a rush, I thought if I turned the toaster level to the highest setting, it would get done quicker. Next thing I knew, the entire kitchen was filled with smoke. By the time the toast popped out, it was a shriveled mess of charcoal, and everything smelled like burnt toast, including me.

With two minutes to spare, I grabbed my backpack and ran to the bus stop. The minute I walked into class, my teacher, Mrs. Schneider, saw that I looked frazzled, with tears starting to form in my eyes. The kids looked at me and laughed. Mrs. Schneider, however, held out her arms, gave me a big hug and sprayed her fancy perfume all over me. That day I learned kindness goes a long way.

Kindness is a leadership skill ... and a life skill

Being kind isn't just a moral choice; it's one of the most effective ways to shape your organization's culture and enhance engagement. Why is this so impactful? Kindness leads to tangible, measurable benefits.

According to the Random Acts of Kindness Foundation, kindness stimulates the release of oxytocin, often called the "love hormone." This substance can lower blood pressure and improve heart health while also boosting self-esteem and fostering optimism. Interestingly, even just witnessing acts of kindness can trigger these positive effects. Imagine how profound the impact is when you actively participate in kind acts.

Also, people who volunteer tend to report fewer aches and pains, and practicing kindness can have health benefits equal to or surpassing those of regular exercise. Acts of kindness also trigger endorphin production, which alleviates pain and discomfort. People who make a habit of practicing kindness show lower levels of cortisol, a hormone linked to stress, compared to the average population.[2]

Acts of kindness not only benefit people's health; they energize people and foster happiness. A study from the Greater Good Science Center at the University of California, Berkeley, found that nearly half of participants felt a surge of energy and strength after helping others. Many reported decreased feelings of depression, increased calmness and a boost in self-worth.[3] In a 2010 survey by Harvard Business School involving 136 countries, researchers found a strong correlation between generosity and happiness — those who give are often the happiest.[4]

As the saying goes, kindness is contagious. As a leader, it's vital to recognize that your actions and treatment of others significantly affect your team's behavior. When people witness or experience your kindness, they gain the benefits mentioned above and are more likely to extend kindness to others, creating a ripple effect both within and outside the organization. Kindness can spread rapidly and profoundly transform your workplace culture.

---

[2] "The Science of Kindness," Random Acts of Kindness Foundation, accessed April 14, 2025, https://www.randomactsofkindness.org/the-science-of-kindness.

[3] Summer Allen, "The Science of Generosity," Greater Good Science Center at the University of California, Berkeley, May 2018, https://ggsc.berkeley.edu/images/uploads/GGSC-JTF_White_Paper-Generosity-FINAL.pdf.

[4] Lara B. Aknin, Christopher P. Barrington-Leigh, Elizabeth W. Dunn, et al., "Prosocial Spending and Well-being: Cross-Cultural Evidence for a Psychological Universal," Harvard Business School, working paper 11-038, accessed April 14, 2025, https://www.hbs.edu/ris/Publication%20Files/11-038_0f1218f0-91b3-4bae-8054-0fca25be5736.pdf.

By identifying opportunities to show kindness and express appreciation, you not only benefit your own health and well-being, but you also contribute to building a collaborative and positive team culture. Let kindness be a key part of your leadership legacy.

Joe Capper: a case in kindness

My friend and colleague Joe Capper, CEO of BioTelemetry from 2010 to 2021 and now CEO and director at MIMEDX, has demonstrated how leading with kindness is best. During the COVID-19 pandemic, his company faced the same challenges as many businesses, with financials trending downward. However, his primary concern was not the company's bottom line but how his employees were coping with the social unrest and uncertainty of the pandemic.

Joe believed that core values must be lived out, not just displayed as words on a wall. To support his team, he arranged for a food service vendor to provide free meals at the front door for all employees. As they shared a meal, Joe would simply ask, "How are you holding up?"

Many of his employees expressed fear about the unrest. Aware that there was no quick solution, Joe responded with transparency and empathy, helping his team envision what getting back to normal could look like. By staying true to the company's values, offering acts of kindness and actively listening, Joe helped his employees see a path forward, even as they navigated the worst of the crisis.

Kindness in crisis

The COVID-19 pandemic was one of the hardest leadership challenges I faced during my career. Everything happened so fast and it impacted everyone — employees, families, patients…everyone. Like many people, I struggled as I tried to keep up with the changes, implement new protocols and disseminate information. I became the Queen of Zoom and held video meetings for the entire organization. Many of those meetings included Q&A sessions with our chief medical officer. This helped to ease people's fears, because our doctor answered questions in real time in easy-to-understand language.

Good leaders can be formed at any time, and great leaders are often formed during a crisis. If you're in a leadership position, your team will turn to you to see how you're handling a crisis. If you stay calm, provide the facts and serve as a trusted source of information, you'll help your team pull together and get through the storm.

During my time leading through crisis, I learned that kindness and compassion are essential tools for supporting people. Simple acts like calling someone to check in or sending a delivered meal became a regular part of my day.

TIFFANY'S TAKEAWAYS

- **Give yourself space to grow.** Spend some time cultivating independence through idleness. Look out the window, sit at a Starbucks, watch people walk by or wait in line without pulling out your phone. The times when it feels like nothing is happening are fertile ground for new ideas, for discovering who you are. Everything today is telling you how to act and who to be, when we really need more time to let our true selves out.

- **Lead with kindness.** If you're wondering how you can lead with more kindness and don't know where to begin, Gary Chapman and Paul White, authors of "The 5 Languages of Appreciation in the Workplace," highlight that people prefer to be recognized in different ways. These include acts of service, quality time, words of affirmation, tangible gifts and appropriate physical touch.[5] Take the time to learn each team member's individual preferences and tailor your approach accordingly.

- **Practice showing appreciation.** Practicing kindness as a leader takes just that — practice. Seek out opportunities to be kind to your team. If you have a standing monthly meeting, pick one thing to do at each meeting to show your team your appreciation. This could be something like treating them to a special lunch, having their cars washed while they're in your meeting or greeting them personally at the lobby door. It doesn't have to be expensive or excessive, just a notably nice thing to do.

---

[5] Gary Chapman and Paul White, *The 5 Languages of Appreciation in the Workplace* (Northfield Publishing, 2012).

Chapter 2

Own Your Uniqueness so You Can Challenge the Status Quo

Leaders who lean into their individuality naturally drive transformation.

Owning our uniqueness is easier said than done, even for leaders. We all long to fit in — to belong — and sometimes that means we diminish the qualities that make us unique. Sometimes we hide who we really are to fit into the box of what we think a leader should be like. But real leaders know their uniqueness can set them apart.

When leaders embrace the qualities that make them unique, they're effortlessly authentic, and that authenticity builds trust. Why? Because people who embrace their authenticity usually have a strong grounding in their values. If those values aren't aligned with the status quo, they'll question the status quo. Leaders who lean into their individuality don't follow the crowd — they set their own rhythm. By breaking away from sometimes-outdated business norms, they naturally drive transformation.

People are drawn to leaders like this — leaders who stand true to genuine beliefs and values. They're also magnetized to these leaders because their authenticity gives everyone else on their teams permission to be themselves. They create a culture of openness and innovation, where people aren't afraid to speak up and share the next great idea. Diversity of thought leads to different perspectives being shared and debated among a team so the best ideas can rise to the top.

"I don't want to play Barbie. I want to make a business plan!"

Since I was a little girl, I've known I'd go into business. When other girls came over to my house to play Barbie, I wanted to play store. At 5 years old, I was learning how to make a profit.

I didn't mind that I was different from the other girls. Being different is cool. Embracing who I truly was from a young age set me up for success in the world of business.

You, just like everyone else, have an individual selling proposition that makes you *you*. That's the gift you have to embrace and develop. Don't try to be like everyone else. Find more opportunities to be you. Accept being different and celebrate your unique, authentic self.

When you were a child, what was different about you? Did you embrace your unique qualities, or did you change to fit in? If you changed, how might you reconnect to the exceptional part of yourself now?

Curiosity: the secret sauce to success

Staying curious in business is crucial because curiosity drives innovation, adaptability and growth. My friend and colleague Derek Maetzold, founder, president and CEO of Castle Biosciences, had a unique journey leading to the creation of his company. He began his career as a pharmaceutical sales representative at Sandoz, where he quickly discovered his passion for learning the technical aspects of medicine — reading scientific literature, understanding pharmacology and discussing patient-centered outcomes. This blend of scientific curiosity and the ability to translate data into meaningful patient benefits became the foundation for his successful startup, Castle Biosciences.

Derek shared with me that he'd never set out to become a CEO. His true passions were research, innovation and creating solutions. He was working on a business plan with The University of Texas MD Anderson Cancer Center to expand its molecular laboratory. The plan ultimately wasn't implemented but the experience sparked his interest. Leveraging what he'd learned, Derek began exploring disease states and cancer indices, focusing on clinical needs and patient benefits and convincing doctors of the role new diagnostics could play in improving the accuracy of their treatment plan decisions — a formula that became his "secret sauce."

Starting Castle Biosciences came with significant challenges, from securing funding to finding a laboratory and building a team. Yet Derek's hard work, market insights and relentless drive to make a positive patient impact left a lasting impression on those who worked with him. Operating on a shoestring budget, he assembled a core team and got creative with operations through contracting and goodwill. He began bringing in samples to provide critical clinical diagnostic information — laying the groundwork for the company's success.

Castle Biosciences Common Stock (CSTL) is traded on the Nasdaq Stock Market with revenues exceeding $300 million in early 2025.

Tesla: disrupting the automotive industry

Tesla has revolutionized the automotive and energy industries through its innovative approaches to electric vehicles (EVs), renewable energy and autonomous driving technologies.

Founded in 2003, Tesla aimed to prove that electric vehicles could be superior to gasoline-powered cars in terms of performance, safety and convenience. At a time when the automotive industry was dominated by combustion engine vehicles, Tesla's mission was both ambitious and unconventional.

While EVs already existed before Tesla, they were often limited in range and performance. Tesla's introduction of the Roadster in 2008, followed by models like the Model S, Model 3 and Model X, demonstrated that EVs could offer long ranges, rapid acceleration and advanced features, challenging perceptions about electric cars and raising the standards.

Tesla also adopted a direct sales model, selling vehicles online and through company-owned showrooms, bypassing traditional dealership networks. This approach allowed for greater control over the customer experience and pricing, disrupting the conventional car sales model.

Tesla invested heavily in developing Autopilot, its advanced driver-assistance system, pushing the boundaries of autonomous driving capabilities and prompting competitors to accelerate their own autonomous vehicle programs.

Beyond automobiles, Tesla expanded into energy storage and generation with products like the Powerwall, Powerpack and Solar Roof, aiming to create a sustainable energy ecosystem that integrated seamlessly with its vehicles.

Tesla's innovations compelled traditional automakers to invest in electric vehicle technology and rethink their strategies. The company's market capitalization soared, making it one of the most valuable automakers globally. Tesla's success also spurred advancements in battery technology, charging infrastructure and renewable energy integration.

Tesla's approach exemplifies how challenging established norms can lead to significant industry transformation. By reimagining vehicle design, sales and energy integration, Tesla not only disrupted the automotive sector but also influenced broader shifts toward sustainability and innovation.[6]

Challenging the status quo: asking questions

My good friend Cathy Langham is a successful entrepreneur who started Langham Logistics and has always embraced her true self. Qualities like empathy, active listening and learning from others have been instrumental in her ongoing success. When she was 15, Cathy started her first job at Coney's Restaurant in Indianapolis. She noticed a clear division: girls worked as waitresses while guys worked in the kitchen. Unafraid to question the status quo, she repeatedly asked the owner, "Why can't girls cook?" With persistence, she eventually became the restaurant's first female cook.

Cathy's knack for asking questions in a way that inspires collaboration has been with her since the start. Her ability to challenge norms has paved the way for her success in the trucking and logistics industry. What we learn from Cathy is to ask the uncomfortable questions. You can use this in any situation. Ask the questions that others haven't asked or are afraid to ask. It's how leaders accelerate growth.

Warby Parker: disruption through uniqueness

In 2012, a small startup named Warby Parker emerged in the eyewear industry, challenging established players like Luxottica and others that dominated the market. Co-founders Neil Blumenthal, David Gilboa, Andrew Hunt and Jeffrey Raider recognized a gap in the eyewear market: Glasses were overpriced, and the purchasing experience was cumbersome. Instead of mimicking the conventional retail approach, they decided to leverage

---

[6] Editor, "Being a Challenger Brand — Top 10 Brands That Have Disrupted the Status Quo," *Home Business*, October 13, 2020, https://homebusinessmag.com/businesses/business-spotlights/being-challenger-brand-10-brands-disrupted-status-quo.

their ability to challenge the status quo and asked the questions that challenged the industry's norms.

From the start, Warby Parker was determined to carve out its identity. Through surveys, observations and questions, the company's leaders understood that consumers, especially millennials, valued authenticity, transparency and social responsibility. They embraced these values by developing a business model that not only sold stylish, affordable glasses but also focused on giving back. For every pair of glasses sold, the company donates a pair to someone in need. This initiative, part of Warby Parker's "Buy a Pair, Give a Pair" program, resonates deeply with socially conscious consumers.[7]

But it isn't just a commitment to social good that sets the company apart; it's its approach to retail. Warby Parker introduced a direct-to-consumer model, allowing customers to try on frames at home before making a purchase. This innovation disrupted the traditional eyewear shopping experience, which often involved limited options and high-pressure sales tactics. By sending customers a selection of frames to try on for free, Warby Parker eliminates the intimidation often felt in retail environments.

The company's uniqueness helps it succeed. A few months after launching, the Warby Parker team faced a critical challenge: They needed to increase brand awareness in a crowded market. Rather than sinking money into traditional advertising, they turned to their customer base for creative solutions. They tapped into their customers' personal stories by inviting them to share their experiences on social media, using the hashtag #WarbyParker.

The response was overwhelming. Customers began posting photos of themselves in their new glasses, sharing heartfelt stories about how the

---

[7] "Buy a Pair, Give a Pair," Warby Parker, accessed April 16, 2025, https://www.warbyparker.com/buy-a-pair-give-a-pair.

glasses transformed their lives — whether by improving their confidence at a job interview or enhancing their ability to read to their children. This organic engagement not only created a sense of community but also showcased the brand's values. Warby Parker isn't just selling glasses; the company is part of its customers' narratives.

The strategy paid off. By embracing its uniqueness and encouraging customers to do the same, Warby Parker rapidly gained traction. In just a few years, Warby Parker became a household name, generating over $250 million in revenue by 2015. Warby Parker's commitment to social responsibility and innovative business practices attracted significant attention from investors, leading to a successful round of funding.

Even as it grew, Warby Parker remained committed to its core values. It continued to promote transparency, sharing pricing and production processes with customers, which fostered trust and loyalty. It differentiated itself not just by the product but by the values it embodied.

Today, Warby Parker is often cited as a case study in how to disrupt an industry by owning your uniqueness. The company demonstrates that success doesn't require conforming to established norms; rather, it's about identifying what makes your brand special and amplifying those attributes. Warby Parker's journey illustrates that by understanding your strengths, being authentic and engaging your customers, you can create a powerful connection that transcends mere transactions.

Warby Parker's rise in the eyewear industry is a reminder that when you embrace what makes you different, you have the potential to change the game.

TIFFANY'S TAKEAWAYS

- ◆ **Discover your true self.** Embracing your individuality can make you a great leader. Authenticity builds trust and naturally drives transformation. Don't follow the crowd. Stay true to your values and set your own rhythm.

- ◆ **Learn by asking questions.** What qualities can you leverage to enhance your leadership skills and let your true self shine? Gain insight by asking people you work with and your personal friends a couple of key questions:

    - When you think of me, what are the first three words that come to mind?
    - Why do you enjoy working with me?

    Ask as many people as possible and gather their responses, paying close attention to common themes. For instance, if you consistently hear words like "reliable," "good listener" or "accountable," take note of those traits.

- ◆ **Reinforce your uniqueness.** Congratulations, you now know what makes you one of a kind! If you like what you hear, keep reinforcing your exceptional qualities in all that you do. If you want others to recognize a different quality you have, make sure this quality shines through in your actions. Actions are how you change perception.

💎 **Create a personal hashtag.** A quick and simple way to remind yourself of your special strengths is to create a personal hashtag and use it with pride. My hashtags are #loveteams, #leader, #advisor and #problemsolver. What are yours?

Chapter 3

Implement Ownership Culture

*You don't have to choose between
standing out and lifting others up.*

In Chapter 2, you explored what makes you unique — the traits that set you apart and strengthen your leadership potential. While individuality is powerful, effective leadership also requires a collectivist mindset. Real leaders understand how to balance self-expression with team cohesion by fostering what's known as an "ownership culture."

Ownership culture means every team member feels personally invested in the success of the organization. It's about showing up with integrity, doing your best work even when no one is watching and taking responsibility for outcomes. It's not just about completing tasks — it's about caring deeply about how the work gets done and how it contributes to the bigger picture.

You don't have to choose between standing out and lifting others up. Individuality within a collective framework means bringing your distinct perspective in ways that encourage connection and collaboration. As a leader, your role is to model this mindset and create an environment where ownership is not just encouraged but expected.

When people are empowered to act like owners — trusted, respected and given a voice — they show up differently. Accountability rises, engagement deepens and your team becomes more resilient, motivated and aligned with long-term success. Whether you're leading a team of two or 200, building a culture of ownership starts with you.

Ownership culture can look different depending on your industry, team size and business model, but the essence is always the same: initiative, accountability and pride in contribution. In a startup, ownership might show up as a customer support representative noticing recurring complaints about a product feature and, instead of just logging tickets, taking the initiative to compile data and collaborate directly with the product team to propose a fix. In a larger corporate setting, it might be a project manager taking responsibility for missed deadlines and proposing new systems to prevent repeat issues. In a service-based business, it could be a frontline employee who goes out of their way to ensure a client experience exceeds expectations — because they see the client's satisfaction as part of their own success.

At an organizational level, ownership culture is supported through open communication and shared goals. Leaders should consistently connect daily tasks to the company's mission, so every team member understands the "why" behind their work. Companies that implement employee stock options, profit sharing or performance-based bonuses often do so to reinforce this mindset tangibly — but the real driver is emotional buy-in.

Giving employees autonomy in their decision-making and publicly recognizing individual contributions are simple but powerful ways to reinforce ownership. When employees are treated as trusted stakeholders, they start acting like they are. Ownership culture doesn't require a title or a promotion — it requires a consistent invitation to step up. As a leader, that invitation begins with you.

Not just a job

When I was 15 years old, I got my first real job at Rita's House of Beauty. It was nothing serious, just a part-time gig to make pocket money — or so I thought. I'd ride my bike to the hair salon where I swept floors, washed towels and watched women's hair being feathered in the style of 1970s actress and style icon Farrah Fawcett.

One day, I showed up an hour late for work. I'd been at home listening to rocker Peter Frampton and had completely lost track of time. The shop owner, Rita Olafsson, yelled at me when I was clocking in. "Did you forget there was an entire wedding party getting ready for their big day today?" she said. "Eight women: a bride, four bridesmaids, two mothers and a grandmother!"

Mrs. Olafsson wanted everything to be perfect, and dirty floors, a lack of towels and a sweaty teenager coming in late didn't meet her idea of perfection.

Until then, it had never occurred to me that, although my job didn't feel significant to me, it played an important role in Mrs. Olafsson's business — and in her customers' lives. My experience taught me that everyone counts; every person who works for you is part of your success.

This stuck with me, even when I was leading big teams as CEO. I'd learned that ownership culture means every team member feels personally invested in the business of the organization, even if their job is washing towels and sweeping up hair so patrons can emerge with perfect Farrah flips.

As a leader, it's your job to develop a sense of ownership with your team. To accomplish this, you need to first make sure everyone understands their role and how it impacts the larger organization and its mission. In the case of my salon job, the atmosphere, how clean the area was, how the towels were folded and the feelings customers wanted to experience when they entered the salon — that was the mission and vision I eventually owned. I learned to be more mindful of others and their time. Beauty salons are not about getting your hair done; they're about the power of transformation, and I had an important part to play in that transformation.

Results = success

My good friend Ann Murtlow, the former CEO of both United Way of Central Indiana and Indianapolis Power & Light (now AES Indiana) who is active on several boards, took her father's advice all of the way to the top. Her dad had a simple philosophy: "No participation medals. You get 2 points for trying and 98 for succeeding." This approach shaped her path to becoming a successful CEO in both the public utility and nonprofit sectors and as the parent of two successful adult children. She learned early that achieving success meant producing real results, taking ownership of her work and bringing value. Trying hard is all well and good, but if it doesn't yield results, success will be elusive. Ann's father, Paul Dragoumis, was a nuclear engineer with a master's degree in philosophy who served as an executive officer at a Washington, D.C.-based utility. He set clear expectations, especially around professionalism in the workplace.

His advice? If you don't know what's expected, find out — and then deliver. He maintained that the only thing that brings success is results, and you can't compromise your values (i.e., no cheating). How you get there matters … a lot.

As a leader, Ann employed this same philosophy in all her companies. She instilled a culture where ownership had three key ingredients: responsibility, accountability and metrics. Her formula? Making sure that jobs were designed for the employee to be both responsible and accountable. Metrics, key to helping people understand if they're winning, were tied to external benchmarking and internal key performance indicators.

Ann's advice: Be careful in matrix organizations, a complex organizational structure where employees often have dual reporting relationships. If they're not structured carefully, matrix organizations can unintentionally make people responsible but not accountable. Not only is that a recipe for ambiguity, but it also can lead to a lack of personal ownership. If you're truly responsible, you own both your successes and your failures, as well as the responsibility for owning and fixing what went wrong. In this scenario, pride is built, success is attained, everyone in the organization learns something and the organization is the beneficiary of current and future successes.

Leading change without losing people

We've all experienced it: the conflict that arises when one person prefers the status quo and another wants to take a risk and go for something new. I ran into this at home when I wanted to renovate — a project I believed would add value to our house — but my husband was perfectly content with things the way they were. We couldn't move forward without being aligned. The same dynamic plays out all the time at work, especially when you're the one championing change.

At work, you could be tasked with shepherding a change that others don't like: a new product line, a global expansion or entering a new market.

In either case, you can't reach your goal alone. You need to overcome resistance and convince others to join you. So, how do you create an ownership culture to make the change happen? Let me explain with a real-life leadership story.

A true story of transformational leadership

It was my first day on the job. My role involved launching a new division. Whenever I begin a new leadership position, I start with listening, and what I heard from my team were statements like, "The old way is working" and "You don't understand. Why would we expand?" I didn't exactly hear "Why won't she go away?" but I heard something close to it!

When you're leading a big change initiative, you're selling an opinion — an idea. Launching this new division was going to be my biggest sale ever.

To reach my goal, I went back to my roots in sales. My solution included three key steps that helped me change a culture, add a profitable new line of business and demonstrate my value as a leader.

My first step was to map out all of the people who had a stake in the change. I noted people's potential motivations for supporting our new division. Who would be sold by potential profitability and market share? Who would be sold by technology and science? Then I drilled down deeper using categories I learned about from Tom Searcy of Hunt Big Sales.[8] These included:

- **The sponsors** who really wanted the change to happen and saw the value in what I was doing.
- **The leaders** in direct power who I needed on my side (division presidents).
- **The angels** in indirect power positions who could influence others.
- **The friends** who were willing to help and support me.
- **The spies** who were just watching what I was up to and reporting back.
- **The eels,** smiling villains who'd try to make the project fail. (They may never go away, but their voices can be neutralized.)

Once I figured out who all the players were, I mapped out my plan on a piece of paper. I knew I needed to move people into the "friendly" box — the space that would lead to advocating for change-encouraging transformation.

---

[8] "5 Steps to Solid Strategic Planning," *Hunt Big Sales*, accessed September 12, 2025, https://www.huntbigsales.com/blog/5-steps-to-solid-strategic-planning/.

Before I could truly lead, I needed to understand the emotions behind people's resistance to change. So I went on a listening-and-learning tour to find out what was behind their resistance and determine if I could minimize their fear.

I prepared for conversations by asking myself questions like, "Why should they care?" and "How will the change I'm proposing make things better?" I tried to put myself in their shoes and ask questions to address their hopes, vulnerabilities and fears, such as, "Imagine you had more money, time and control. What would you do?" and "What if this new way could get you there?"

The listening process helped me refine my stakeholder map. I discovered who believed the change would lead to a better future, who was ready to work with me — and who I still needed to convince.

Shepherding change requires you to win not only people's hearts but people's minds. My listening tour helped me build an emotional connection with my stakeholders. The next step was to win their minds. This allowed them to have ownership in the change.

When you're trying to convince people, especially scientists and engineers, data and graphics win the day. So, I sought out third-party case studies and stories known in the industry to show factually what could be done. Armed with information, I was ready for a road show. I gave presentations and had conversations that helped pique people's interest in the change.

As employees adopted the new idea, even on a small scale, we celebrated. When the new idea started to work, we celebrated loudly. Soon others wanted to learn what was working so well and how they could be involved.

It takes time to overcome objections through listening, building trust and winning your team members' hearts and minds. But it's worth it. Today, the new way of working I helped introduce is not only accepted at that company; it's part of the way business is done — and it's profitable, too.

My home renovation didn't turn out so bad, either, and I'm still happily married. When you shepherd change by listening, learning and leading, you preserve valuable relationships, both at work and at home.

Not just a beer

New Belgium Brewing kicked off the microbrew culture in Colorado with its flagship product, Fat Tire. Co-founder Kim Jordan attributes the company's values to her previous career as a social worker.[9] Every employee earns a New Belgium-branded bicycle on their first anniversary with the company as a tradition that reflects its ownership culture.

In 2012 and until its sale in 2019, New Belgium became a 100% employee-owned company through its employee stock ownership plan. Through open-book management, employees were given access to company financials and trained to understand them. This shaped how the employees thought about the company and its mission and helped make Fat Tire one of the most successful microbrews in the United States.[10]

Employees' individual performance directly influenced their earnings. It transformed them into more productive employees — and brand ambassadors.

---

[9] "Our Story," New Belgium Brewing, accessed April 18, 2025, https://www.newbelgium.com/company/story/.
[10] Tanza Loudenback, "Why the Maker of Fat Tire Bucked the Trend and Became 100% Owned by its Workers," June 13, 2016, *Business Insider*, https://www.businessinsider.com/new-belgium-brewing-kim-jordan-2016-6?utm.

TIFFANY'S TAKEAWAYS

- 💎 **Maintain a professional presence.** To reflect the values and seriousness of your company, present yourself professionally. When you're at work, dress for work. Don't show up in pajamas with messy hair on a video call — being online doesn't mean you can project an unprofessional image. Take charge of how you're seen. This is the crucial first step.

- 💎 **Clarify your goals.** To build an ownership culture, make sure your goals are clear. Provide space for the people on your team to ask questions and discuss how they can contribute meaningfully to each goal. The metrics you use and track should be directly tied to the goals and behavior you're trying to instill.

- 💎 **Learn from your customers.** The best way to find out if your team members are taking true ownership and accountability for their work and outcomes? Ask your customers — internal and external. How did they feel about their experience? Did they feel valued? Was the product or service up to their standards? These insights will show whether your team is committed to delivering excellence. If there's room for improvement, gather your team, share the feedback and work together to find solutions.

Chapter 4

Embrace the Journey

*The key to navigating leadership lies in
how we respond to challenges.*

When you're a leader, the path to success is rarely a straight line; it's a winding road filled with peaks, valleys and unexpected turns. The key to navigating leadership lies in how we respond to challenges. There will always be surprises and bumps along the way. It's not about avoiding them — it's about learning how to handle them and sometimes even leaning into them. The real growth happens along the way — all the curves, rough patches, slowdowns and accelerations are where leaders are forged. As 19th century preacher, essayist and poet Ralph Waldo Emerson said, "It's not the destination; it's the journey."

In Chapter 1, we explored resilience as a leadership quality rooted in cultivating independence — the ability to stand tall when things get shaky, to take initiative when the path forward isn't clear. In this chapter, we're going to discover why resilience is more than just a personal trait — it's a leadership necessity, especially in times of uncertainty, disruption or change.

Resilience is what allows leaders to remain calm and effective under pressure. It's not about being unshaken or emotionless — it's about maintaining composure and clarity, especially when others start to panic. Resilient leaders don't crumble when things go sideways; they adapt. They look for the lesson in the failure, the opportunity in the obstacle and the next move in the moment of uncertainty. They model what it means to stay grounded and focused, even when plans fall apart.

When a team sees their leader navigating uncertainty with courage and creativity, they're more likely to stay engaged and solution oriented. Resilience becomes contagious. It creates a culture where setbacks don't signal defeat — they signal a challenge to rise to.

Resilience also shows up in small, everyday moments. It's in the decision to show up fully even when you're tired. It's in taking ownership of a mistake and using it as a chance to improve. It's in maintaining hope and vision when progress is slow. And most importantly, it's in believing in your mission — and in your people — even when doubt creeps in.

Real leadership isn't about having all the answers. It's about having the strength to keep going, to adapt, to grow — and to bring others with you. Resilience is the internal armor that allows you to do just that.

A growth mindset

Embracing the journey, with all its ups and downs, is essential for success in both business and life. It's a well-known fact that resilience, adaptability and a positive mindset in the face of challenges lead to better outcomes and personal growth. Even if you don't feel particularly resilient, you can build your skills. Psychological research has shown that the resources and skills associated with greater resilience can be cultivated and practiced.[11]

---

[11] Laura Copley, "Resilience Theory: Core Concepts & Research Insights," PositivePsychology.com, August 22, 2025, https://positivepsychology.com/resilience-theory/.

A study described in the Harvard Business Review found that leaders who embrace uncertainty and stay adaptable during tough times are 30% more likely to lead successful teams.[12] One of the key reasons behind this finding is that challenges often lead to growth. Carol Dweck, a Stanford University psychologist, introduced the concept of the "growth mindset," which posits that individuals who see challenges as opportunities to learn and grow are far more successful than those who have a "fixed mindset" and avoid adversity. Dweck's research shows that people with a growth mindset are not only more resilient but are also 50% more likely to push through setbacks and achieve long-term success.[13]

Resilience is increasingly becoming one of the most sought-after leadership qualities, with management consulting firm McKinsey & Company reporting that 75% of executives view adaptability as a critical factor in leadership effectiveness.[14] So what does resilience actually look like in business and leadership?

If at first you don't succeed: insights from global leaders

In business, companies that embrace change and learn from mistakes thrive in the long run. Jeff Bezos, the founder of Amazon, famously said, "If you double the number of experiments you do per year, you're going to double your inventiveness. Failure and invention are inseparable twins."

---

[12] Timothy R. Clark, "What Employees Need from Leaders in Uncertain Times," *Harvard Business Review*, February 28, 2024, https://hbr.org/2024/02/what-employees-need-from-leaders-in-uncertain-times.

[13] Carol Dweck, "Carol Dweck Revisits the 'Growth Mindset,'" *Education Week*, September 22, 2015, https://www.edweek.org/leadership/opinion-carol-dweck-revisits-the-growth-mindset/2015/09.

[14] Jacqueline Brassey, Aaron De Smet, Ashish Kothari, et al., "Future Proof: Solving the 'Adaptability Paradox' for the Long Term," McKinsey & Company, August 2, 2021, https://www.mckinsey.com/capabilities/people-and-organizational-performance/our-insights/future-proof-solving-the-adaptability-paradox-for-the-long-term.

Bezos' perspective is rooted in the understanding that the journey, with all its failures, is integral to innovation and growth. Research shows that by embracing the journey — the setbacks, the learning curves and the victories — you not only grow stronger but also more adaptable, creative and, ultimately, successful.[15]

Many leaders have faced challenges on their paths. Howard Schultz, former CEO of The Starbucks Coffee Company, grew up in a poor neighborhood and faced numerous rejections when trying to secure funding for his vision of transforming the coffee experience. Instead of letting these setbacks deter him, he adapted his approach, focusing on building relationships and articulating his vision clearly. Schultz's ability to navigate through obstacles not only shaped Starbucks into a global brand but also illustrates the importance of resilience in leadership.[16]

Another resilient leader is Ratan Tata, former chairman of Tata Sons. Tata faced numerous hurdles when trying to enter the competitive automobile market with the Tata Nano, a low-cost car aimed at middle class families. This inexpensive, four-seat, rear-engine hatchback was first produced in 2008 in India, geared to motorcycle and scooter drivers, for 100,000 rupees (approximately $2,500 in U.S. dollars at the time).[17]

The project encountered technical difficulties and production delays, and many doubted its feasibility. Yet Ratan Tata remained steadfast, adapting the strategy based on feedback and learning from each setback. His perseverance and willingness to pivot ultimately led to the Nano's launch,

---

[15] Jeff Bezos, "Fireside Chat," speech, Washington, D.C., May 5, 2017. Internet Association 2017 Annual Charity Gala.

[16] Tanza Loudenback, "How Starbucks Founder Howard Schultz Went from Rags to Riches," *Inc.*, October 22, 2015, https://www.inc.com/business-insider/rags-to-riches-story-of-howard-schultz.html.

[17] Richard S. Chang, "Tata Nano: The World's Cheapest Car," *The New York Times,* January 10, 2008, https://archive.nytimes.com/wheels.blogs.nytimes.com/2008/01/10/tata-nano-the-worlds-cheapest-car/.

showcasing that a leader's journey involves continuous learning and adaptation. Eventually, in 2018, the Tata Nano was discontinued, but the lessons learned from this project were never forgotten and are used in other areas of the business.[18]

When the journey gets rough…

My friend Rod Cotton, a recognized business leader and former senior vice president, chief of staff and head of strategy and transformation at Roche Diagnostics, felt a self-pep talk is exactly what he needed after an early career promotion. He'd been promoted from field sales to the corporate office at a major pharmaceutical company's global headquarters. This move presented him with the chance for further growth and advancement if he could prove himself. Rod had been in his new role only for a short time when he received his first review — and it wasn't good. He'd thought he was doing well but realized there was a lot to learn about navigating office politics and effective communication within a global organization.

Following the review, Rod went into the restroom to take a moment to encourage himself. He mentally reinforced his strengths — his capability, hard work and resilience — reminding himself he could handle anything that came his way. Reflecting on the tougher challenges he'd already conquered, he resolved to adapt and thrive in this new environment. With a renewed sense of determination, he emerged with a fresh perspective and outlook that set him up for success.

Over the years, Rod has continued to give himself pep talks to boost his confidence. As part of his process, he uses an unusual, highly effective tool:

---

[18] Ratan Tata, "India car boss Ratan Tata admits Tata Nano 'mistakes,'" BBC, January 5, 2012, https://www.bbc.com/news/world-asia-india-16427707.

the embodiment gesture. (See "Power poses" in Chapter 9 for a different take on building confidence through physical gestures.)

Rod explained that an embodiment gesture is a physical cue — it could be a color or a strain of music or a hand gesture — that keeps your vision and goals front of mind. You summon it when facing situations that make you feel like you can't succeed or you're not good enough.

"Your gesture could be a simple movement, like raising your fist in the air. It could even be imagining raising your fist in the air," Rod said. "When you accompany the gesture with a phrase to give yourself courage, like 'I've got this,' it can make you feel even more empowered.

"Nobody has to know about your gesture," Rod said. "It's your own personal reminder to sustain your self-confidence, keep your vision in focus and show up as your best and brightest self."

My Janesville moment

When I was graduating from the University of Minnesota in Minneapolis, I had the opportunity to interview with Cargill's Nutrena Feed Division. As a naive college student, I borrowed my mother's skirt and $20 and set off on what I thought would be a straightforward journey. Cargill covered my travel, and my plan was to fly from Minneapolis to Chicago and then from Chicago to Janesville, Wisconsin.

When my flight finally reached Chicago, I had only five minutes to go from Terminal C to Terminal F to make my small commuter flight to Janesville. When I reached my gate, my flight had just taken off. "Now what?" I thought. Here I was, stranded in Chicago with only $20, and I didn't know what to do. All I knew was I couldn't miss my interview.

I noticed another flight that was boarding and going to Madison, Wisconsin. "Same state — how far could it possibly be from Janesville?" I thought. This was a 20-seat plane and, as we proceeded to take off, I started a conversation with the people around me, including the pilot. I told them how I desperately needed to get to Janesville for my first on-site interview, which included dinner that night. I had no money, no credit card, and I really couldn't stay in Madison.

"Would it be possible to simply drop me off in Janesville?" I asked. I was young, naive — and bold. I really didn't want to miss the interview. Being naive is sometimes a gift because you're not encumbered by what is; you only think about what could be. And sometimes, asking is exactly what you need to do. The whole plane voted to make an unexpected stop in Janesville. Yay, problem solved! I felt like I was living all I had learned from my mother and my work experience up until that point: Be on time, be prepared and don't let anything stop you.

I landed at 10 p.m. The airport was dark, with only one 60-watt bulb hanging over a "Do Not Enter" sign on the door. I banged on the door. A janitor opened it, and we both waved goodbye to the plane. After landing in Janesville, I discovered my adventure had just begun. The interviewers weren't there to meet me. They thought I was stuck in Chicago and were en route there to pick me up — a two-hour drive one way. This was in the time before cell phones. With hours to kill, I turned a potentially frustrating situation into an opportunity for self-reflection and learning. As I sat in the empty airport, I realized that every leader faces moments of uncertainty and discomfort. It's in these moments that we must dig deep, find our own "Janesville moments" and demonstrate our capacity to adapt.

At 1 a.m., the interviewers finally picked me up. It was late, no one had eaten, and we still needed to do the interview. We proceeded to the only place that was open in town — a Pizza Hut. I was grilled for the next hour over pepperoni and sausage pizza. A week later, they offered me the job.

Since turning the plane around and doing what it took to accomplish the goal — in my case, getting to Janesville for my interview — what I learned is that sometimes you need to take control of the momentum, move forward and change the circumstances. In other words, dig in and fight.

Don't let your assumptions get in the way of brainstorming or dreaming about positive outcomes. When you have nothing but a goal, reaching it can take moxie, creativity and a bit of luck. Seize your own "Janesville moments."

TIFFANY'S TAKEAWAYS

- ◆ **Break goals into actionable steps.** Start by clearly defining your goal — whether it's for a new project, an upcoming meeting or a career move like joining a board. Write it down and break it into actionable steps. For example, if your goal is to serve on a board, your roadmap might include completing board training, crafting a tailored board resume and actively networking for opportunities. Be as detailed as possible in defining your goal, setting clear milestones along the way. Then, place your written goal somewhere regularly visible to keep it top of mind and in focus.

- ◆ **Embrace the detours on your path.** When unexpected challenges arise, revisit your goal. If you're not on the path you envisioned, ask yourself: "Will this path still help me get where I want to go?" The journey might take longer or look different, but as long as it moves you toward your destination, it's still progress. Don't give up. Seize the moment!

- ◆ **Give yourself a pep talk.** When things aren't going your way, pause and take a moment to gather your thoughts. Reflect on the challenges you've overcome in the past and your ability to do so again. Remind yourself of your goals and your determination to meet them. Develop a physical cue — it could be a color or a strain of music or a hand gesture — that keeps your vision and goals front of mind. Summon your cue when you face challenging situations.

Chapter 5

Put the Customer First, Not the Numbers

The best insights come from stories, not spreadsheets.

We've all heard the phrase, "The customer comes first." It's plastered across websites, signs and storefronts and recited in TV ads. But do most businesses really put customers first? Unfortunately, and especially in larger corporations, internal metrics, which are much easier to control, measure and report, take center stage. While these metrics are important, they don't represent the full picture. They're not the same as a clear understanding of whether or not a customer is satisfied with the results you've delivered and what you could do better from the customer's perspective.

Real leaders understand that the best insights come from stories, not spreadsheets. They seek out honest customer feedback and testimonials and then strive to do better based on this information. Their metrics point to the most important aspects of the business, not what's easiest to measure. They realize that putting the customer first should be much more than just a slogan.

"Learn the customer and you'll learn the business."

When I held a role as general manager of a home healthcare company, visiting our customers/patients was essential to understanding how we were doing. Everything was pointing to success.

One sunny morning, I jumped up on the porch of a house and rang the bell. I was confident, feeling good about the business metrics I'd been tracking, eager for the opportunity to talk with customers one on one and ready to meet my first customer of the day.

On this particular day, I planned to visit Elizabeth, a new mom with a 6-month-old baby using a ventilator. I wanted to hear firsthand how fabulous we were and then be on my way to all my other meetings. But Elizabeth didn't think we were so fabulous. I ended up staying the rest of the afternoon. "I'm not happy," she said. That simple, cutting statement stopped me in my tracks.

Elizabeth shared how every time she tried to order routine supplies for her baby, she was put on hold. We'd lose her previous orders, transfer her repeatedly and then she'd get disconnected. Here was a mother caring for a sick child while we — despite hitting all our numbers — were completely failing her.

It dawned on me that metrics can be misleading, or worse, irrelevant if they don't reflect the actual customer experience. On paper, we looked perfect. But to Elizabeth, none of our performance statistics mattered. All she cared about was that she couldn't rely on us in her time of need. Suddenly, I realized I had been managing to the metrics, not leading with a bigger vision. My focus had been on numbers, not people, and I had lost sight of what truly mattered.

This reminded me of something my grandfather once told me. He was a successful entrepreneur and, during a lunch conversation early in my career, I asked him what the secret to running a good business was. He smiled and said, "Learn the customer, and you'll learn the business. It doesn't matter what kind of business you're in — if you understand the customer, you'll be the most valuable person in the company." He stressed that success wasn't about sales techniques or slick marketing campaigns — it was about listening to the customer. "Ask them about their pain points," he said, "and figure out what they really need, not what you think they need." That advice had stayed with me, but until my conversation with Elizabeth, I hadn't fully grasped its significance.

That day taught me something powerful: Leadership is about putting the customer first, not the metrics. You can hit every goal, exceed every benchmark and still fail spectacularly if you lose sight of the people behind those metrics. Numbers don't tell the full story — only the customer can. When Elizabeth told me how (literally) disconnected and frustrated she felt, I knew immediately that our focus had been wrong. We weren't measuring what truly mattered.

Cases in excellent customer service

Apple: unspoken customer needs

When it comes to customers, Apple really does excel. Steve Jobs, while developing the iPod, didn't rely on surveys or endless data. He famously said, "People don't know what they want until you show it to them."[19] That's because Jobs understood that the true key to leadership isn't data — it's deeply understanding the customer's unspoken needs. Jobs didn't ask customers for feedback on incremental improvements; he created products that revolutionized their lives because he knew, instinctively, what they really wanted. His focus wasn't

---

[19] Jason Aten, "This Is Steve Jobs's Most Controversial Legacy. It Is Also His Most Brilliant," *Inc.*, January 19, 2021, https://www.inc.com/jason-aten/this-was-steve-jobs-most-controversial-legacy-it-was-also-his-most-brilliant.html.

on what could be measured at the time; it was on crafting an experience that would resonate with people on a deep, personal level.

Southwest Airlines: The business of business is people

Similarly, Herb Kelleher, the co-founder of Southwest Airlines, built his entire business on the principle of putting people first. He once said, "The business of business is people — yesterday, today and forever."[20]

Kelleher didn't care about traditional airline metrics like how many seats were filled or how many flights took off on time. Kelleher focused on making sure every customer felt valued and every employee felt empowered to make that happen. By doing so, he built one of the most loyal customer bases in the airline industry. His leadership was never about data or metrics — it was about the human connection.

Zappos: going above and beyond

Another great example of the putting-the-customer-before-the-numbers approach is in the story of Zappos, the online shoe retailer founded by Nick Swinmurn and later led by Tony Hsieh. From the beginning, Zappos was focused on providing exceptional customer service, even at the expense of short-term profits. Hsieh, as CEO, believed that building a strong, customer-centric culture was the key to long-term success. He didn't just want satisfied customers; he wanted loyal, raving fans.

Zappos became known for its extraordinary customer service, going above and beyond to ensure customers were not only happy but amazed by their

---

[20] Linda Rutherford, "Farewell to Southwest's Founder," Southwest Newsroom, January 3, 2019, https://www.swamedia.com/southwest-stories/farewell-to-southwest-s-founder-MC722OCVPR-R5CJHMZG376CBONU4U.

experience. One of the most famous examples is when a customer service representative spent 10 hours on a single call with a customer.[21]

The call wasn't just about selling shoes; it was about creating a genuine human connection and helping the customer feel heard and valued. While such an interaction might seem unprofitable from a purely financial perspective, Zappos saw these moments as key to building long-term loyalty.

Hsieh implemented a 365-day return policy and offered free shipping both ways, which at the time seemed financially risky and could have hurt the company's bottom line. Many companies would see these policies as unnecessary costs. However, by focusing on the customer's needs and eliminating friction in the shopping process, Zappos gained trust, repeat business and word-of-mouth referrals that catapulted the company to success.[22]

The proof is in the results. Under Hsieh's leadership, Zappos grew from a small startup to a billion dollar company in less than a decade. The decision to put customers ahead of immediate profits proved sustainable when Amazon acquired Zappos for $1.2 billion in 2009. Even after the acquisition, Zappos maintained its customer-first philosophy, staying true to the values that built the brand.[23]

Hsieh often emphasized that customer service shouldn't just be a department but instead the entire company. His leadership demonstrated that when companies focus on making customers happy, successful financial results will follow naturally.

---

[21] Zappos.com, "10 hours 43 mins: The Longest Customer Service Phone Call @ Zappos," February 21, 2017, YouTube, 1 min., 19 sec., February 21, 2017, https://www.youtube.com/watch?v=PloPddCWAjE.

[22] Chris Guillebeau, "Selling Service and Shoes: Interview with Tony Hsieh of Zappos.com," The Art of Nonconformity, accessed April 21, 2025, https://archive.chrisguillebeau.com/selling-service-and-shoes-interview-with-tony-hsieh-of-zapposcom.

[23] Simone Baribeau, "How Tony Hsieh Pivoted Zappos into a $1.2 Billion Amazon Acquisition," Fast Company, September 4, 2012, https://www.fastcompany.com/3000591/how-tony-hsieh-pivoted-zappos-12-billion-amazon-acquisition.

Nordstrom: a long-term strategy

I love the Nordstrom story about obsession with exceptional customer service and have shared it often in meetings. The story starts almost 40 years ago at a Nordstrom store in Fairbanks, Alaska. A customer walked into the store with two used tires asking for a refund, despite Nordstrom never selling tires. It had, however, years before bought stores from Northern Commercial of Alaska, which had sold tires. Instead of rejecting the customer, the Nordstrom store associate called a tire company to value the tires and issued a refund. Nordstrom now hangs tires in its stores as a customer service reminder. In fact, this story has reached mythical status in Nordstrom lore and continues to get millions of hits.[24]

You might think, "Ouch, that'll mess up your profit for the day." But what's so brilliant about the story is that it's long-term thinking, and long-term thinking is about building relationships with your customers. This story is about reinforcing the salesclerk's empowerment to make decisions to keep the customer happy and reinforcing the behavior and culture you want modeled. It's about all employees doing what it takes. In Nordstrom's case, commitment to 100% customer service was and is the best strategy.

The Ford Pinto: a cautionary tale

What does it look like when you don't put the customer first? Have you heard of the Ford Pinto case from the 1970s? It reveals what happens when numbers become more important than the customer. Ford rushed the Pinto to market, knowing it had a serious design flaw that made the gas tank prone to explosion in rear-end collisions. But instead of addressing the problem, the company calculated that it would be cheaper to settle lawsuits for wrongful

---

[24] Nordstrom, "The Nordy Pod: The Truth About Nordstrom's Legendary Tire Story," Nordstrom Now, accessed August 12, 2025, https://press.nordstrom.com/news-releases/news-release-details/nordy-pod-truth-about-nordstroms-legendary-tire-story.

deaths than to redesign the vehicle. Ford was too focused on the numbers, prioritizing cost saving over customer safety. The result? People died. In addition to a tragedy, the company faced a public relations disaster, numerous lawsuits and a permanent injury to Ford's reputation.[25] It's a chilling example of what happens when metrics overrule ethics and customer trust.

Managing versus leading

All these stories drive home the same lesson I learned that afternoon with Elizabeth, the new mom. Leadership is not only about hitting targets or following metrics; it's about understanding and prioritizing the customer's experience. When you truly listen to the customer, you'll know what needs to improve and what needs to be celebrated. You can't lead by just managing numbers — you lead by knowing your customers deeply and caring about their experience above all else.

Elizabeth just wanted to feel like she and her infant mattered, that she wasn't simply a number on our spreadsheet. She wanted the human touch, and I needed to learn to lead, not just manage.

Management and leadership are two completely different skill sets. (There's a reason we use the phrase "micromanager" but never "microleader.") Managers are supposed to get into the nitty-gritty. Leaders are supposed to see the big picture. Their job is to make their vision so clear to others that they see it, too, and work toward that goal. Hitting metrics and understanding the big picture are two totally different things. I learned that I was managing in a leadership role when I should've been leading. I wasn't making sure we were measuring what mattered and letting people know the story behind the metrics. We were missing our big WHY!

---

[25] Aaron Gold, "The History (and Tragedy) of the Ford Pinto: Everything You Need to Know," *Motor Trend* magazine, April 4, 2024, https://www.motortrend.com/features/ford-pinto.

Early in my career, I watched a manager storm into a meeting, furious that the people on her team hadn't hit their monthly targets. She shouted, "There's the door if you don't want to be here!" It was demoralizing for everyone on the team, many of whom had been working long hours and weekends. She was so focused on the numbers that she had completely lost touch with her people. That day, she lost the respect of her team, and she never regained it. Leaders who focus solely on metrics can lose not only the customer but also their teams. And a leader without a team will be lost.

Metrics are important, yes, but they're only tools. The trick is to make sure they are measuring the right things. They should never overshadow the human experience. The real goal is creating an interaction that leaves your customers feeling valued, heard and connected. If you lose sight of that, no amount of data will save you. My conversation with Elizabeth was a wake-up call — a reminder that no metric could measure the frustration of a mother who just needed to feel heard and cared for.

When you prioritize your customer's needs, the numbers will follow, but if you chase metrics without considering the people behind them, you'll fail every time.

Putting the customer first

When your customers are patients — especially patients battling cancer — putting them first isn't just good practice; it's the foundation of your business. My friend and colleague Derek Maetzold, founder, president and CEO of Castle Biosciences, built his company with that principle at its core.

With a professional background in rare cancers and personal experiences involving friends and family affected by them, Derek was driven to create a company focused on diagnostic testing for underserved populations. He started by identifying rare diseases with significant unmet clinical needs. Treatment decisions were being made without the benefit of good diagnostic tests to guide those decisions, and he wanted to change that. This approach provided two opportunities.

First, focusing on cancers with smaller patient populations meant working closely with the limited number of medical experts in each field — so a clinician base could be reached with a small commercial investment. Collaborating with these specialists helped solidify the clinical need as well as garner early support from key opinion leaders. Second, it meant limited diagnostic competition, as established laboratories can't profitability scale down while a startup like Castle can be right sized from the beginning.

Eighteen years later, Castle Biosciences has expanded its testing pipeline across dermatology, gastroenterology and ophthalmology. The success of the company stands as proof that putting the customer first is the most powerful business strategy there is.

Centering the customer: a formula for lasting success

My good friend Cathy Langham, CEO of Langham Logistics, understands that putting the customer first is the cornerstone of lasting success. She describes her strongest teams as those united by a shared vision — one focused on delivering exceptional value to the customer. That vision extends beyond individual roles or company goals; the team succeeds only when the customer succeeds.

When Langham Logistics began truly partnering with its customers, that vision grew stronger. By actively listening to customers' needs and challenges, the company was able to develop tailored solutions — including building custom warehouses and offering specialized services designed around each client's specific requirements.

From a small startup to a thriving logistics company more than 30 years later, Langham Logistics is proof of what can happen when you align your team around the customer, shape your offerings with their input and treat their success as your own. It's the power of partnership — and the power of putting the customer at the center of everything you do.

How to put the customer first

Become the customer's advocate. Regardless of your role — whether you're a CEO or an entry-level employee — your customer can provide you with the insight you need to improve.

Even if you're in a position like finance, IT or human resources, you still have customers; they're internal customers. A customer-first philosophy can apply to both external and internal customers. Customer feedback will tell you what you should continue doing, what you should change and what you should start doing.

The next time you speak with an external customer, start with these three questions:

1. How would you rate us compared to the competition?
2. Why do you choose to buy from us?
3. Have you experienced any pain points with our company? Could you tell me about them?

If you have internal customers, your questions could be:

1. Do you get your information from us in a timely manner?
2. Are we easy to use and do we understand your goals?
3. Have you experienced any pain points with us? Could you tell me about them?

Keep in mind that how you ask the questions is important. Some customers may prefer to keep their comments confidential, while others might be open to a personal interview.

Relevance is key

My son Kevin's pet peeve is when a company asks you to take a survey, but they ask the wrong questions. He recently saw a phone service company advertising a special that included a free iPhone watch, a new phone at a discount and a lower internet fee. The offer was for both new and current customers. As a current customer, and knowing the value of the deal, Kevin went to one of the company's local brick-and-mortar locations. The service was great — he walked out with his watch, phone and lower monthly rate.

And then the first monthly bill arrived. Not only did the company fail to apply the lower rate, but it actually increased his monthly payment and charged him full price for both the watch and the iPhone. Kevin went back to the store, where a new associate "fixed the problem."

Afterward, he received a survey with the question: "Would you hire the person who helped you?" His answer was yes — they were friendly and did their best. But the real issue was the company's system, not the employee. There was no way for Kevin to give the company the feedback it really needed.

The next month, the billing issues still weren't fixed. After a two-hour phone call, Kevin was told he'd have to contact the company every month to get someone to manually correct the bill. Needless to say, he wasn't a happy customer!

Measuring the wrong metrics will not get you loyal customers — or the answers you need to improve your business. When your customers are willing to give you their opinion, make sure you're asking the right questions.

TIFFANY'S TAKEAWAYS

- **Listen to your customers.** Start by asking your customers about their experience and then listen. Really listen. Don't focus on defending your company or the metrics you've hit. Ask relevant questions that get to the real issues. Refer to the section in this chapter titled "How to put the customer first" as a starting point for creating questions that move your business forward.

- **Take action to meet customers' needs.** Become the most valuable person in your company by translating what the customer needs and identifying how you can meet those needs. Bring the customer (their views and opinions, that is) into your meetings. It doesn't matter where you sit in the organization; you can still solicit feedback and carry the voice of the customer back to your company.

- **Let customer feedback drive your decisions.** You'll find that what matters most to customers rarely shows up in a spreadsheet.

CHAPTER 6

You Can't Succeed Alone

Growth doesn't happen in comfort zones.

Leadership is often associated with independence, but that stereotype is far from reality. Real leadership is rooted in collaboration, both in the workplace and behind the scenes at home. Leaders can't (and shouldn't) do everything on their own. We are social creatures, designed to rely on our support networks.

Getting the support you need requires humility — because you have to ask for help. Good leaders recognize that other people sometimes have the expertise they lack. Leaders also must be willing to give help selflessly, because sometimes what's required isn't necessarily a stepping stone to the top of the ladder. While many of us have an image of leadership rooted in power, authority and supremacy, many leaders are humble helpers both at work and at home.

Asking for help

It was 6 p.m. The dog was barking, the microwave was buzzing and my son needed a pirate costume by tomorrow. Amid this domestic chaos, my phone rang with news of a manufacturing disaster at work. In that moment, I was pulled in all directions, a reality familiar to anyone balancing family and a demanding career. It reminded me that no matter how hard you try to handle everything, sometimes you simply can't — and that's OK.

Welcome to the world of juggling family and professional work. While it never has been easy and never will be, I'll share with you some things that helped me. But first I need to share a little background.

I met my husband, Brad, while I was an undergraduate at the University of Minnesota. We'd both responded to an ad that a ski resort in Crested Butte, Colorado, had placed in the school newspaper: "Are you sick of school? Do you love to ski? If you answered 'yes' to both questions, come interview for a job at our resort." Brad and I were among eight students who landed jobs in Crested Butte. We didn't know each other when we both took a semester off to spend a ski season in Colorado. Working at the resort was like living in a dorm without schoolwork. Brad and I became close friends, and six months after we returned to the university, we started dating. We married in 1986 and stayed in Minneapolis. Brad worked in medical sales, and I sold pharmaceuticals in Minnesota, Iowa and Wisconsin.

In 1998, Brad and I made a significant life decision: to move from Minneapolis to Indianapolis for a role I'd been recruited for at Roche Diagnostics. At the time, it was unconventional for a woman to have the more prominent job, but Brad was fully supportive. We had long, deep conversations about what the move would mean. Communication became the cornerstone of our success. It wasn't just about moving houses; it was about openly discussing what we wanted out of life and work. Being honest about your goals and sacrifices, whether with your partner or your colleagues, is critical.

The job itself was a big opportunity — a leadership role at Roche's corporate office, which was crucial for career growth in those days. Being close to the C-suite meant visibility and visibility meant promotions. We both knew, though, that the biggest challenge wasn't the new job; it was uprooting our entire family, including our daughter, Jess, and our son, Kevin. We'd leave behind friends, routines and even the perfect neighborhood coffee shop, where the barista knew my order by heart. But through that discomfort, I realized something critical: Growth doesn't happen in comfort zones. Moving taught us all — especially our kids — about flexibility and how embracing new situations, even when they're difficult, leads to incredible opportunities.

I made a list and started to figure out what I needed to move forward. Through writing, I began to understand issues on a deeper level. This move was less about the uncertainty of the decision and more about the enormous list of things that needed to get done.

First on my list was to find a neighborhood, not just any location, to move. We wanted a neighborhood filled with young families like ours where we could find instant friends. Community has always been important to me. I wanted to live in a place where the neighbors care for each other, watch over the property and the children and help each other. I wanted a neighborhood where "just ask" is as common as the extra burger at the barbecue. They say it takes a village to raise a child and it's true. Putting in the time to find the right neighborhood would save us time down the line, and I found it in the Bayhill area in the northern Indianapolis suburb of Carmel. The schools were great and there were lots of families and kids in our age bracket. It turned out to be a perfect fit.

I continued to add the practical things I needed to my list, but I instinctively knew there was something I couldn't quite put my finger on. You see, being self-sufficient from an early age means asking for help has always been difficult for me.

Esther Perel in her podcast "How's Work" often asks the question: "Were you raised to be autonomous or to be loyal?" She explains these two approaches with clear definitions.[26]

Being raised to be autonomous means you were taught that you can only depend on yourself and no one else can assist you as effectively as you can. On the other hand, being raised to value loyalty suggests you were brought up understanding that you're never truly alone and that relying on others for help is both natural and necessary. Perel notes that these aren't rigid categories — you may not have stayed this way into adulthood, but this mindset shaped your upbringing.[27]

This distinction between autonomy and loyalty becomes especially evident in the workplace. Dutch social psychologist Geert Hofstede's research on culture and its influence in organizations touches on this dynamic through the dimension of individualism versus collectivism. His work reveals how these orientations manifest in professional environments.[28]

In my professional life, I've encountered both individualistic and collectivistic tendencies. Those with an individualistic approach, particularly senior team members, often prefer working independently. They believe that only they have the expertise necessary to execute tasks to a high standard. Trusting others with responsibilities can be difficult for them, as they fear

---

[26] Lewis Howes, "Greatness Clips: Autonomy VS Loyalty: Esther Perel," The School of Greatness, accessed August 12, 2025. YouTube, 38 sec., https://www.youtube.com/watch?v=PyOsBDYq2Ls.
[27] Elisabeth Morgan, "Were you raised for autonomy or interdependence? — Esther Perel at CreativeMornings/New York," Medium, November 15, 2019, https://medium.com/%40elisabethsmorgan/were-you-raised-for-autonomy-or-interdependence-6999ee948ce7.
[28] Charlotte Nickerson, "Hofstede's Cultural Dimensions Theory," Simply Psychology, August 13, 2025, https://www.simplypsychology.org/hofstedes-cultural-dimensions-theory.html.

their team won't meet their expectations. However, these individuals often become invaluable sources of expertise, with colleagues regularly seeking them out for advice. Over time, their in-depth knowledge sets them apart, even if they sometimes work in isolation.

In contrast, collectivist leaders tend to foster strong, enduring relationships with their teams. They focus on group success, aiming to benefit the largest number of people, not just themselves. They're energized by helping others and creating environments where collaboration thrives. These individuals often create a "family" atmosphere at work.

Ultimately, whether someone leans toward autonomy or loyalty, both approaches bring strengths and challenges. How we were raised shapes not only our personal lives but also how we interact in professional environments.

For me, it was clear that I had been raised in autonomy and was used to solving problems on my own. That had to change.

Chris Gardner was a highly independent business leader, and his life inspired the film "The Pursuit of Happyness." Gardner, played by Will Smith, faced homelessness while raising his young son. Despite his independent spirit and determination, he acknowledged the importance of seeking help when it came to raising his child safely.

He requested shelter from the Rev. Cecil Williams at Glide Memorial Church in San Francisco and Williams agreed without hesitation. This act of seeking help allowed Gardner the stability he needed to pursue a career in finance. Eventually, he became a stockbroker and founded a brokerage firm, Gardner Rich, LLC, in 1987. Gardner's journey highlights that even the most determined individuals benefit from support during challenging times.[29]

---

[29] Chris Gardner, *The Pursuit of Happyness* (Amistad Press, HarperCollins Publishers, 2006), Kindle edition, 2024, 10.

So, I asked for help — from friends, from colleagues, even from our 60-year-old babysitter, who graciously agreed to move with us for a short time (which turned into three years). That simple act of asking changed everything. I'd been so focused on carrying the load myself, I'd forgotten that people actually want to help, if only you'll let them.

That brings me to the most unexpected lesson I learned: Asking for help is a strength, not a weakness. I'd always been fiercely independent, but during that move, I realized I couldn't do it all on my own.

Courageous conversations

I frequently listen to the podcast "How I Built This" with Guy Raz, who interviews the world's best-known entrepreneurs to learn how they built their iconic brands. You hear how they started, their inspiration and what went wrong. Sometimes it's a question of scale, sometimes a poor decision, but what I always hear is who helped them come up with the solution. It's rare that someone does it all on their own. Sometimes it's their work partners, sometimes it's their life partners, sometimes it's an advisor or friend.[30] Success is made with teams, and asking for help is a sign of strength.

My advice to you is, don't try to do it all on your own. If you aren't already partnered up, find someone who you can communicate with about everything. Find a partner who will work with you to realize your dreams. If you're already in a relationship and feel as though you're lacking in this area, work on this with your partner!

This is the basis for all good relationships in both your personal and professional life. Be courageous and have those conversations one sometimes forgets to have when stressed and caught up in daily life. What does work mean to you? How much are you willing to sacrifice? Is your goal

---

[30] "Guy Raz Official Site," Guy Raz, accessed September 14, 2025, https://www.guyraz.com/.

security, freedom, flexibility, more responsibility? For me, my dream was to lead and create. When we moved to Indianapolis, I was just coming into my stride and wanted the opportunity to grow and to give.

I'm so grateful my family supported me. I also supported them by asking questions like: What's important? How are you feeling? What's difficult? How's it going? Establishing a healthy and open channel of communication between me, Brad and our kids served us well when we moved to Indianapolis and it would come into play further down the road.

Ben & Jerry: a dynamic duo

Ben Cohen and Jerry Greenfield's journey from leading a small startup to an iconic ice cream brand showcases the importance of partnership, collaboration and seeking help from others to achieve success.

In 1978, childhood friends Cohen and Greenfield decided to turn their passion for food into a business. With little knowledge about making ice cream, they took a $5 correspondence course on ice cream from Penn State University and converted an old gas station in Burlington, Vermont, into their first scoop shop. They didn't have a lot of money or experience, but they relied on their partnership, each bringing different strengths to the table. Cohen, who had a limited sense of taste and smell due to a medical condition, focused on the texture and feel of the ice cream while Greenfield handled the business side of things.

The early years were tough. Cohen and Greenfield had to learn about the complexities of running a business from the ground up. They faced challenges with scaling the business, distribution and competing with much larger brands like Häagen-Dazs. When Ben & Jerry's was still a small-scale operation, Cohen would answer the phone pretending he was an assistant. When someone made an order, he said his driver would deliver. The driver was Greenfield in a baseball cap. They worked this way for a while but quickly realized they couldn't do it all themselves. Instead of trying to manage every aspect of the business alone, they brought in outside help, forming strategic partnerships and leaning on their community for support.

One pivotal moment came in 1984 when Häagen-Dazs, owned by Pillsbury, tried to prevent their distributors from selling Ben & Jerry's ice cream. Rather than fighting this battle on their own, Cohen and Greenfield turned to their customers and community for help. They launched a grassroots campaign called "What's the doughboy afraid of?" to rally support. "Our customers — those who loved our ice cream — were the ones who would truly feel the impact if Ben & Jerry's went under," Cohen said. With this perspective, he and Greenfield devised a bold strategy to engage their fans directly. They adorned each pint of ice cream with a sticker that proclaimed "What's the doughboy afraid of?" and included a toll-free phone number for people to call and hear their story about Pillsbury's attempts to stifle them.[31, 32]

Encouraging customer involvement, they offered a "doughboy kit" for anyone who reached out. This kit featured a letter template titled "Why don't you pick on someone your own size?" meant for the chairperson of Pillsbury, a letter to the Federal Trade Commission, a bumper sticker bearing the same catchy phrase and the chance to purchase a $10 T-shirt emblazoned with "Ben & Jerry's Legal Defense Fund: Major Contributor." This grassroots effort had a Kickstarter-like flair, showcasing Cohen and Greenfield's innovative thinking long before crowdfunding became mainstream.

The response was astounding. "We began receiving around 100 calls daily on that line, mainly during the late-night hours — prime ice cream time,"

---

[31] "6 (Almost) Scandals from Ben & Jerry's History," Ben & Jerry's, accessed April 21, 2025, https://www.benjerry.com/whats-new/2016/6-almost-scandals.
[32] Art Basmajian, "What's the Doughboy Afraid Of?" Barron Marketing, December 17, 2018, https://barronmarketingsolutions.com/whats-the-doughboy-afraid-of/.

Cohen recalled in an article he wrote titled "The Definition of Business."[33] The chairperson of Pillsbury was swamped with correspondence and the conversation surrounding the company's anti-competitive tactics gained momentum. Significant features appeared in respected publications like The New Yorker, The Boston Globe Sunday Magazine, the Hartford Courant, The Wall Street Journal and The New York Times. This public pressure forced Pillsbury to back down, allowing Ben & Jerry's to continue growing.

Another example of collaboration was when Ben & Jerry's sought to balance its rapid growth with its commitment to social responsibility. Cohen and Greenfield brought in professionals like Jeff Furman, a longtime friend, to help draft the company's mission statement and design an innovative business model that balanced profit with purpose.

They also established the Ben & Jerry's Foundation to give back to the community, making sure that social values were embedded in the company's business structure.

Cohen and Greenfield knew they needed a broader team of people to manage the company's growth, and, in 1994, they handed over the CEO role to Robert Holland Jr., an experienced leader, to help them navigate the complexities of managing a much larger enterprise. This decision reflected their understanding that while they were creative and passionate, they couldn't take the company to the next level on their own.

By the time Cohen and Greenfield sold their company to Unilever in 2000, it had grown into a globally recognized brand, known not only for its quirky flavors but also for its dedication to social causes. Through every step of their journey, Cohen and Greenfield knew they couldn't succeed alone. They relied

---

[33] Ben Cohen, "The Definition of Business," *Innovations: Technology, Governance, Globalization*, Volume 6, Issue 2, April 1, 2011, https://direct.mit.edu/itgg/article/6/2/3/9656/The-Definition-of-Business.

on each other, their employees, their community and external experts to help them build a sustainable business that reflected their values.

As Cohen once said, "Business has the responsibility to give back to the community. You can't operate in a vacuum."[34]

Finding balance by leaning on others

I've learned throughout my career that teamwork and support lead to greater success than doing it all on your own.

Early in my career, I noticed that no one talked about their kids at work, especially not women. It was seen as a sign of weakness if you had to leave early to take care of a sick child or attend a school event. There was an unspoken rule that family responsibilities should stay in the background, far away from the office. Despite the progress we've made toward gender equality, this tension between work and family persists and it was made even more evident during the COVID-19 pandemic.

When the pandemic hit and daycare centers closed, it was predominantly women who found themselves juggling work with childcare and homeschooling. A 2021 study found that more than 2.3 million women in the United States had left the workforce during the pandemic, with many citing the demands of childcare as the primary reason. Women were disproportionately impacted, taking on the lion's share of domestic duties while also trying to maintain their careers. The result was enormous stress, exhaustion and, in many cases, burnout. For lots of us, it felt like no matter how hard we tried, we were falling short, both at work and at home.[35]

---

[34] "Ben Cohen and Jerry Greenfield: Caring Capitalists," *Entrepreneur*, October 10, 2008, https://www.entrepreneur.com/growing-a-business/ben-cohen-and-jerry-greenfield/197626.
[35] Jonathan Rothwell and Lydia Saad, "How Have U.S. Working Women Fared During the Pandemic?" Gallup, March 8, 2021, https://news.gallup.com/poll/330533/working-women-fared-during-pandemic.aspx.

Making the dream work

For much of my life, I've prided myself on being independent and getting things done alone. But as my responsibilities grew, I learned that success isn't achieved alone. You need a team, both professionally and personally. The importance of relying on others — at home and at work — cannot be overstated. If you want to be a strong and effective leader, it's essential that you cultivate a support system.

During the early years of my career, I never talked about my family life at work. I never talked about the challenges of being a mother and having a full-time leadership job. At my kids' school, I was never the teacher's helper or the volunteer who baked cakes or went with the class on field trips. I was the one who sent in paper plates and napkins. Whenever I could go to a school play or baseball game, of course, I did but it's hard managing it all and can often feel like you're coming up short everywhere.

When I faced challenges with balancing my family and career, my support system helped guide me. I developed a close circle of colleagues both inside and outside of my company and industry who knew how deeply I cared for my family. Many of them had families as well. There was empathy all around for what people were going through. Within my company team, way before mental health days, we'd give each other a "free pass" to leave early or come in a bit late when life obligations required attention. Sometimes all we needed was the support of colleagues who understood our situation to help us feel comfortable with making those choices.

My husband, Brad, has been there for me and our family at every stage of my career. I know I've been lucky to have such a supportive partner. Another woman who achieved success thanks to her husband is Facebook's former Chief Operating Officer Sheryl Sandberg. She's often cited for her advocacy of women's leadership, but what's less known is how Sandberg credits much of her success to the support system she built. She has spoken openly about how she relied on her late husband, Dave Goldberg, for both personal and professional advice. In fact, Sandberg has said that her husband's emotional support and willingness to take on an equal share of parenting duties allowed her to thrive at Facebook and beyond.[36] Her story is a testament to the fact that we can't do it all on our own and that leaning on others isn't a weakness, it's a strength — especially when you choose a supportive partner.

Collaboration and leaning in

There's a significant amount of research that supports a collaborative approach to leadership. Studies show that organizations with inclusive and collaborative cultures — where team members feel empowered to ask for help — are more innovative and successful in the long run. A study by Deloitte found that companies with inclusive cultures are twice as likely to meet or exceed financial targets and six times more likely to be innovative. These statistics highlight the power of teamwork and collaboration, something that can be achieved only when leaders are willing to admit they can't do it all alone.[37]

As you move into senior leadership positions, you'll need to recognize when you need help. You'll also need to rely on your team, so make sure you build a strong one. (See Chapter 7 for tips on building a supportive team and earning buy-in).

---

[36] Emily Crockett, "How the death of Sheryl Sandberg's husband made her rethink Lean In," Vox, May 9, 2016, https://www.vox.com/2016/5/9/11640052/sheryl-sandberg-lean-in-husbands-death-single-mom-facebook.

[37] Juliet Bourke and Bernadette Dillon, "The Diversity and Inclusion Revolution: Eight Powerful Truths," *Deloitte Review*, Issue 22, January 2018, https://www2.deloitte.com/content/dam/insights/us/articles/4209_Diversity-and-inclusion-revolution/DI_Diversity-and-inclusion-revolution.pdf.

When I was promoted to a senior leadership role that was far more complex than anything I'd done before, it was nerve-racking. The stakes were high, and I felt completely out of my depth. But instead of trying to handle everything myself, I opened up to my team and shared my challenges. I asked for team members' input, sought advice from mentors and delegated responsibilities to people I trusted. The result? The goals were met, and I grew more as a leader than I ever could have if I'd tried to take it all on by myself.

Sometimes leadership isn't linear

This idea of relying on others and giving back became a core principle of how I wanted to lead.

Once I'd established myself at the corporate office of Roche Diagnostics, a new role opened: vice president of molecular diagnostics. It wasn't a more prestigious title than the one I already had, but it was a broader opportunity — with more responsibility and more growth possibilities. In business, growth doesn't always come with a promotion; it often comes with new experiences that challenge you in unexpected ways. Leadership is about seizing opportunities to learn, even when the reward isn't immediate.

There are countless examples of military leaders making lateral moves in order to gain more technical or combat experience. Usually these moves are intentional, but sometimes a leader's best work can come from unexpected circumstances, especially when they rely on their team for help.

One such example is David Marquet, a retired U.S. Navy captain who's now a leadership expert. In the late 1990s, Marquet trained to command the USS Olympia, a nuclear-powered attack submarine. However, he was reassigned to command the USS Santa Fe. This was a lateral move, not a promotion, and he was unfamiliar with this particular submarine class. He had to completely adapt his usual leadership style to account for his knowledge gaps, giving his crew more control and encouraging them to take the initiative. This decision transformed the USS Santa Fe from one of the worst-performing submarines in the fleet to one of the best. Marquet achieved top rankings in performance and retention. Not only did his submarine overperform; many of his crew members went on to achieve leadership positions themselves.[38]

Leaders help in small but important ways

Leadership sometimes means giving the shirt off your own back, as the adage goes. One day, at a large company meeting, I noticed that Christina, a new associate, was in tears in the restroom — she had spilled coffee all over her blouse and had to give her very first big presentation. Without hesitation, I took off my blazer and gave it to her to cover up the stain. That moment taught me a crucial leadership lesson: Real leaders step in and help, even in the smallest of ways. It wasn't about the blazer; it was about being there for someone in a moment of need. That small act of kindness left a lasting impression on Christina — and me.

Leadership is often associated with having a big ego, so I tell aspiring leaders to stay grounded. Always remember where you came from. Early in her career and after receiving a major promotion, Indra Nooyi, former CEO of PepsiCo, came home late at night and excitedly shared the news with her mother. Her mother listened and then said, "That's great. Now go get some milk." Nooyi later reflected on how this moment reminded her that even in leadership, it's important to stay grounded and take care of the small, human needs that tie us all together.[39]

---

[38] Kevin Kruise, "Leadership Tips From Nuclear Submarine Commander David Marquet," LeadX, Podcast #013, 22 min., 20 sec., March 22, 2017, https://leadx.org/articles/013-marquet/.

[39] "'Can you go get milk?' Indra Nooyi Uncrowned at Home," Brut India, Footage: Aspen Institute 2014, posted January 20, 2021, YouTube, 5 min., 28 sec., https://www.youtube.com/watch?v=dphK7K9zwOA.

Family first

My friend and colleague Derek Maetzold, founder, president and CEO of Castle Biosciences, had been offered a remarkable opportunity at Sandoz's global headquarters in Basel, Switzerland — a move that would open doors to senior leadership and position him for a promising future within the company. It was a chance most people only dream of and it came with the expectation of more moves to other global offices over time. But the decision to accept wasn't as easy as it seemed.

Derek's wife, Sharon, was hesitant from the start. They had four young children, all rooted in their routines and communities, and both sets of their parents, while still living, were in declining health and needed their support. Sharon worried about the strain that moving to another continent would place on their family. They both knew the move would be life-changing but not without sacrifices and, after many discussions, Sharon gave him a gentle but firm "no."

Derek realized that even though passing on this opportunity might hurt his professional record at Sandoz, family had to come first. He decided to turn down the transfer.

Just when he was feeling uncertain about his next steps, Derek came across an opportunity with Dan Bradbury, a life sciences leader who's now a managing member of BioBrit, a life sciences consulting and investment firm in La Jolla, California. Dan would later not only invest in Derek's startup but become the chairman of the board. Derek was offered a new position in San Diego. It seemed ideal at first, with a fresh role and the prospect of living in a vibrant city in California, but when he and Sharon crunched the numbers, reality set in. Between the cost of schools, housing and overall expenses, the gap between the lifestyle they wanted and what they could afford was just too big to ignore.

So, Derek and Sharon decided to take a step back and map out what they truly wanted for their family. They laid out their goals, identifying regions that offered a good balance of opportunity, affordability and a strong sense of community. With this clear picture, Derek and Dan Bradbury explored a more flexible work and commute arrangement. After some negotiations, they agreed on a creative setup that allowed Derek to take on the role without uprooting his family.

That same open communication and family-centered decision-making eventually led Derek and Sharon to Texas. There, they found not only the right environment for their family but also the spark for a new venture. Inspired by his experiences and challenges, Derek founded Castle Biosciences, a place where he could make a meaningful impact while keeping his family's needs at the forefront.

In the end, Derek found a sense of balance and fulfillment he hadn't expected. He'd learned that sometimes the right path isn't the one that looks best on paper but the one that keeps you true to your values and to those you care about most.

Celebrate your contributions

Family balance is tough, especially for working women with children. When my good friend Ann Murtlow was CEO of Indianapolis Power & Light Company (now AES Indiana), she understood the critical role women play in supporting one another in the workplace. She created a local network of more than 50 women in high-level leadership positions — CEOs, presidents, senior vice presidents, chief financial officers and others — and launched a monthly Girls' Night Out group, affectionately known as GNO. These gatherings, which I often attended, were informal, were usually at someone's house and were a way to share ideas, commiserate, exchange advice, support each other and, of course, enjoy some good wine and food.

One evening, the conversation turned to the guilt many of us were facing. Nearly everyone in the group admitted to struggling with balancing family with professional obligations — except one person. She confidently shared, "I'm a better mother because I have a career. I prioritize and manage my time effectively, and my kids see our values in action."

Her perspective shifted the narrative, focusing on the positive impact of working mothers rather than the sacrifices made. It was a powerful reminder to celebrate what we contribute rather than dwell on what we're missing. I approach my life with a similar perspective, and I feel good about how my kids, Jess and Kevin, have become independent and strong thanks to all of the opportunities and experiences my career brought to our family.

Whether you're moving your family across the country, building a career or leading a team, you can't succeed alone. Relying on others is key to your long-term success as a leader. Communicate, ask for help and build strong relationships and a support network. Success isn't just about personal achievement; it's about lifting others up and allowing them to lift you. When you embrace that reality, both personal and professional success become not only possible but inevitable.

TIFFANY'S TAKEAWAYS

- ◆ **Build a network of friends and colleagues.** Asking for help can be challenging, but building a strong network of friends and colleagues with whom you feel comfortable seeking support is a great place to start. A safe and trusting environment is crucial for problem-solving and growth. Cultivate one by stepping in to help others and asking for help when you need it.

- ◆ **Join a professional group.** Consider joining a group of business professionals where open information sharing is encouraged. I was part of a forum for many years where six individuals from different industries met monthly for a few hours to discuss business challenges. This forum created a space to share experiences and seek advice, often leading to better solutions — someone had usually encountered a similar issue before. If you can't find a forum, try starting your own and experience the benefits of asking for help.

- ◆ **Stay true to your values.** Balancing work and your personal life is always a juggling act, and the stakes become higher when your work becomes more demanding. There may be times you need to say "no" to a promotion or transfer. Stay grounded in your values, and make the right decisions at the right time.

- ◆ **Focus on the positive.** Don't let cultural expectations or others' opinions stop you from celebrating your accomplishments both at work and at home.

Chapter 7

Take Risks (as a Team)

*People don't follow perfection.
They follow authenticity and courage.*

Real leadership isn't about choosing what's easy and predictable. It's about stepping into uncertainty, making difficult decisions and being willing to learn through setbacks.

Comfort zones may feel safe, but they often lead to stagnation. Progress — whether personal or professional — requires calculated risk. Innovation, growth and meaningful change all come with an element of uncertainty.

A leader who avoids risk limits forward momentum. People don't follow perfection. They follow authenticity and courage. They follow those who can articulate a clear vision and are willing to pursue it, even without guaranteed outcomes.

But risk is never just a solo effort. Teamwork plays a critical role in smart risk-taking. When leaders cultivate strong, collaborative teams built on trust and open communication, bold decisions become more informed and more effective. Teamwork transforms risk into opportunity.

True leadership isn't about avoiding failure — it's about modeling resilience, adaptability and the ability to lead through complexity. With the right team beside them, leaders can navigate uncertainty and drive meaningful progress.

A risk can change everything

I learned early not to be afraid to take risks. It's easy to feel paralyzed by fear or hesitation but, instead of letting those emotions hold you back, use them to push yourself forward. Getting outside of your comfort zone is where the real growth happens. It's through risks that we discover what we're made of, develop new skills and learn how to solve new problems. The things that scare us often lead to the most growth; that statement has been a guiding principle throughout my career and personal life.

One of my first experiences with this came in eighth grade. I had a choice between a science elective or an English elective. I wasn't particularly interested in science at the time, but all of the cute boys were taking science class. So, I took a risk and chose the science course, not knowing what to expect. As it turned out, I didn't get to know the boys very well, but something far more important happened: I discovered a passion for science that has stayed with me and shaped the trajectory of my career.

Netflix: revolution through risk

When Reed Hastings co-founded Netflix in 1997, the company started as a DVD rent-by-mail service, competing with giant video rental chains like Blockbuster. However, the real turning point came in the early 2000s when Hastings made the bold decision to pivot from physical DVD rentals to streaming, a move that easily could have led to Netflix's downfall.

In the mid-2000s, DVD rentals were still the dominant form of home entertainment, and the internet infrastructure was not fully ready for streaming video. Streaming high-quality content successfully required a much stronger internet connection than most people had. Netflix had built a booming DVD rent-by-mail service, and it would have been safer to stick with that model. But Hastings saw the future. He understood that consumer preferences were shifting, and people wanted instant access to entertainment without waiting for DVDs to arrive in the mail.

The decision to invest heavily in developing streaming technology was a massive risk. It required huge capital investments in licensing content, building a robust platform and upgrading infrastructure — all while alienating a customer base that had grown accustomed to the traditional rental model. Netflix also had to convince content creators and studios to trust the internet as a viable distribution method. Many doubted whether the technology would take off, especially as broadband penetration was still low in many areas.

But Hastings believed in the long-term vision. In 2007, Netflix launched its streaming service, offering subscribers a library of films and TV shows available to watch instantly online. Initially, it faced significant challenges — limited content, technical issues and skepticism from investors. However, Hastings' calculated risk paid off as internet speeds improved and consumer behavior shifted. By embracing streaming early, Netflix positioned itself to ride the wave of digital transformation in media.

Today, Netflix is a global powerhouse, with more than 300 million subscribers in 2024.

This risk not only revolutionized how people consume entertainment but also forced an entire industry to evolve. The company's willingness to take a massive gamble on streaming helped it grow from a niche DVD rental service into one of the biggest content platforms in the world. It took another risk more recently, creating its own content to compete with the traditional movie studios. As of 2025, Netflix has accumulated 26 Academy Awards across narrative feature films, documentaries and shorts, with that number continuing to rise each awards season. The leaders at Netflix aren't afraid to take risks.[40, 41]

The risks we take, no matter how seemingly insignificant at the time, often set the stage for greater opportunities down the road. That science elective in eighth grade was the first of many moments in my life where stepping outside of my comfort zone led to unexpected and transformative results. I eventually built a career that has included numerous leadership positions in science-heavy industries. One of the most important things I learned was that I didn't need to be the smartest person in the room to succeed.

My role as a leader wasn't to have all of the answers but to guide a team that could collectively find those answers. As a leader, it's vital to ask the right questions, respect the expertise of others and be vulnerable when you don't know something. This openness to learning and collaboration is what fosters true growth.

Spanx: Sara Blakely's big risk

In the late 1990s, Sara Blakely was selling fax machines door to door when she experienced a fashion frustration that sparked an entrepreneurial idea. Blakely was preparing to wear white pants for a party and realized that her underwear was creating visible panty lines. Traditional control-top pantyhose weren't a good fix — the pantyhose showed through her open-toed shoes, a fashion faux pas. Plus, full pantyhose were hot and uncomfortable in warm weather.

---

[40] "The Story of Netflix," Netflix, accessed August 12, 2025, https://about.netflix.com/en/leadership.
[41] "Netflix Awards Catalog: Complete List of Academy Award, Emmy, Golden Globe and BAFTA Wins and Nominations," Netflix, accessed August 12, 2025, https://about.netflix.com/en/news/netflix-awards-database-complete-list-of-academy-award-r-emmy-r-and-bafta.

So, in a moment of DIY brilliance, she took a pair of control-top pantyhose, cut off the feet and wore them as shapewear under her pants. The result? Smooth lines, no visible underwear, no awkward toe seams. Suddenly, a whole new product category was born.[42]

What made Blakely's idea so revolutionary was that no one in the hosiery industry was thinking this way — control-top pantyhose traditionally were designed as a full stocking, with little innovation focused on discreet, practical wearability. The market was dominated by large manufacturers that hadn't prioritized women's real-world needs for style and comfort in all seasons.

Blakely saw an opportunity to create something new: a product that was both functional and flattering, giving women confidence and freedom in their clothing choices. Blakely had no background in fashion, manufacturing or business. She didn't have any investors or industry connections. But she did have $5,000 in savings. She took a huge risk and poured all of it into turning her idea into a product — filing the patent herself, cold-calling manufacturers (most of whom dismissed her) and writing her own packaging copy.

After two years of grinding and rejection, she convinced a hosiery mill in North Carolina to make a prototype. She then persuaded a Neiman Marcus buyer to give her 10 minutes. During the pitch, she literally went into the bathroom and modeled Spanx on herself to show the difference.

It worked. Spanx got on the shelves and quickly took off. Oprah Winfrey put Spanx on her "Oprah's Favorite Things 2000" list and sales exploded. Blakely never took outside investment and remained the sole owner. In 2012, she became the youngest self-made female billionaire in the United States.

---

[42] "OurStory," Spanx, accessed June 2, 2025, https://spanx.com/pages/about-us.

Blakely did everything on her own, from product development to sales. Her bold risk didn't just launch a business — it created an entire market and turned her into a global business icon.[43]

Risk-taking: a team effort

As a young U.S. Navy lieutenant, my friend and colleague Joe Capper, CEO of MIMEDX and a leader of several other successful healthcare companies, had received one of his toughest assignments yet: leading a group of very young men in his squadron who were not yet a team. The Navy has a fierce internal competition known as the Battle Efficiency (or Battle "E") awards, and Joe's team was the lowest ranked.

Determined to turn things around, Joe knew he had to build trust and a strong bond with his team. He committed to supporting the soldiers through tough challenges, even if it meant sacrificing his weekends for grueling training exercises. Joe was there every step of the way, offering guidance and standing by them when things got difficult, both during training and in the off hours. In the end, their hard work paid off — they won two Battle "E" awards, sparking a new sense of confidence in each team member and across the squadron. The soldiers in the squad learned to rely on each other as a team, to never give up and to take a risk on themselves. As a result, these same soldiers functioned like a well-oiled machine when they found themselves in live combat a short time later in Operation Desert Storm. They performed at an incredibly high level and, most importantly, everyone returned home safely.

My colleague and friend Rod Cotton's tenure as senior vice president of tissue diagnostics at Roche Diagnostics offers another compelling example

---

[43] Clare O'Connor, "How Sara Blakely of Spanx Turned $5,000 into $1 Billion," *Forbes*, March 14, 2012, https://www.forbes.com/global/2012/0326/billionaires-12-feature-united-states-spanx-sara-blakely-american-booty.html.

of teamwork in action. When the CEO entrusted him with the complex task of integrating a significant company into Roche's multibillion-dollar enterprise, Rod embraced the challenge with his characteristic commitment and determination.

An unexpected loss of a major reimbursement stream just as Rod stepped into his role made the situation even more challenging. The stakes were high. Rod had to navigate 28 separate work streams and lead a team of 40 people. Financial overruns were a concern, and Rod and his team would have to dig deep to meet their financial targets.

How would they succeed?

First, Rod worked to build trust among the people on his team. That required showing up as a leader with openness and vulnerability. "The best way to build trust can also feel like the scariest," Rod said. "Building trust takes time, and it starts with being vulnerable, listening to people and meeting them where they are. When you show your own vulnerability, other people feel more comfortable about speaking up and taking risks."

Empowering a team to take bold steps can require a leader to step back and let people do things their own way — even if they make mistakes. That's where patience comes in. "Sometimes it's hard to be patient with your team, but it's important," Rod said.

In high-stakes situations, it can be challenging to keep your cool, but it's essential that you do. "Your energy can influence others," Rod said. "Even if you don't notice your energy, others will. Not knowing is no excuse."

To manage your energy, especially when you're under pressure, Rod recommends giving yourself time before meetings to clear your head. "When you show up, focus on calmly encouraging and inspiring others to be their best selves," he said. "Stay curious, ask questions and focus on the positive — moving forward, getting better and reaching your goals together."

TIFFANY'S TAKEAWAYS

- **Know the value of taking risks.** Through risks we discover what we're made of, develop new skills and learn how to solve new problems. The things that scare us often lead to the most growth.

- **Get comfortable being uncomfortable.** To grow, we must step out of our comfort zone. It's easy to feel paralyzed by fear or hesitation, but instead of letting those emotions hold you back, use them to push yourself forward.

- **Ease yourself into taking risks.** Taking risks often accelerates personal development. When faced with an opportunity that feels risky, ask yourself: "What's the worst that could happen if I go for it?" For example, when I moved to a different state, my mindset was simple — if we didn't like it, we'd just move back. I applied the same thinking to career changes — if it didn't work out, I'd move on. Trust in yourself and take the chance. This is where real growth happens.

Chapter 8

Prioritize What Matters Most

*Leaders who set clear priorities create cultures
where others can do their best work.*

Real leadership isn't just about managing people — it's about managing priorities. Whether you're leading a team at work or guiding your family at home, your ability to consciously set and uphold priorities defines how effectively you lead.

In our fast-paced lives, it's easy to fall into the trap of reacting to what's urgent rather than prioritizing what's truly important. The squeaky wheel gets the grease — and the demands of work can certainly be loud! However, stepping back and making deliberate choices about where to invest your time, energy and attention is crucial for achieving a sense of balance and fulfillment.

At work, this might look like focusing on high-impact projects instead of getting lost in a flood of email messages. It means being clear about what success looks like, communicating that vision to your team and creating space for deep, meaningful work. Leaders who prioritize well don't just get more done — they create cultures where others can do their best work, too.

At home, conscious priority setting is just as essential. It might mean choosing family dinners over late-night meetings or setting aside time for self-care so you can show up fully present for those you love. It might mean taking time to have fun with friends.

When you lead with your values, you model clarity, purpose and balance. You show others that leadership isn't about doing it all — it's about doing what matters.

Our family command center

Running a family can feel like managing a small business. It requires organization and teamwork. When my kids were still living at home, our family used to gather for a meal every Sunday. We prepared the meal together, from making hamburger patties to setting the table. These dinners were more than just a special meal; they were weekly strategy sessions where we discussed upcoming events, reviewed what had happened in the previous week and celebrated successes — big and small.

Central to our operation was a large whiteboard calendar in the kitchen, our "command center" where everyone's activities and assignments were laid out. This practice was invaluable, and I later found myself applying similar techniques in professional settings. I began to ask my teams the same questions we discussed at home: "What's upcoming and what happened last week that impacted us?"

Our family gathering and regular team meetings were similar to the lean practices[44] employed at my company, Roche Diagnostic Corporation: daily standup meetings that included a whiteboard of current activities, what was already accomplished and what needed attention. These practices were part of the successful running of the business — and they had the same impact on my family.

Blending best practices from home and work allowed me to feel less divided and more integrated in my roles. After all, the common denominator in both spheres of your life is you.

Lean practices: standup meetings and visual metrics

Two foundational practices of lean methodology are daily standup meetings and a visual display of metrics. A daily standup is a short, focused meeting in which members stand to reinforce brevity, hence the name. In this meeting, team members gather to share progress and report potential issues. These meetings serve several purposes. They promote communication through sharing what each team member is working on. They encourage accountability through goal setting, reinforce responsibility for following through and address problems early by discussing issues in real time. They also drive continuous improvement through conversations on process, patterns and recurring issues. Standups are most effective when they're consistent, time limited and focused on progress rather than simply providing status updates.

Lean practices emphasize making key information visible to everyone at a glance. Displaying real-time metrics helps the team make data-driven

---

[44] "What is Lean?" Lean Enterprise Institute, accessed September 14, 2025, https://www.lean.org/explore-lean/what-is-lean/.

decisions and stay aligned with goals. When everyone can see the same data, it fosters trust and shared understanding. Teams also can readily spot issues and self-correct or improve.

How to prioritize: strategies for success

Knowing how to prioritize is essential for staying ahead of deadlines and recognizing when to delegate tasks. There are numerous methods that can help with prioritization. One simple but powerful strategy is the WIN approach, inspired by legendary Notre Dame football coach Lou Holtz. WIN stands for "What's Important Now?"[45]

This principle emphasizes that we achieve our goals step by step, making choices that align with our immediate priorities. It's a reminder that not every task is equally urgent or significant and that focusing on what truly matters can streamline our efforts.

Another helpful tool is the Eisenhower Matrix, which divides tasks into four quadrants:[46]

---

[45] Lou Holtz, *Wins, Losses and Lessons: An Autobiography* (Harper Entertainment, 2024), p. 194, Kindle edition.
[46] Nick Hobson, "69 Years Ago, President Eisenhower Came Up With the Best Matrix for Making Better Decisions," *Inc.,* May 20, 2023, https://www.inc.com/nick-hobson/69-years-ago-president-eisenhower-came-up-with-best-matrix-for-making-better-decisions.html.

EISENHOWER MATRIX

This method helps clarify what demands immediate attention and what can be planned for later, delegated or even eliminated altogether. As we navigate the blurred lines between work and personal life — especially in a world where many of us work from home — this framework becomes even more valuable.

Boundary setting

Consider this: During the COVID-19 pandemic, many people found themselves juggling work responsibilities alongside family obligations, often leading to increased stress and burnout. Statistics from the American Psychological Association indicate that nearly 80% of adults reported a rise in stress due to the pandemic, with working mothers bearing a disproportionate burden.[47]

To effectively manage stress, it's essential to set boundaries. Clearly communicate your availability to colleagues and supervisors so they know when you're reachable and how best to contact you. While emergencies may arise, most matters can wait until regular work hours resume. When your workday ends, put your laptop and smartphone away — out of sight, out of mind.

In a global company, you work with people from different countries and in different time zones, so there's always someone working. Feeling like you need to be "on" 24-7 can create burnout. In one international company, when the senior management team sends email messages, they include a simple statement: "My workday may look different to your workday. Please do not feel obligated to respond outside of your normal working hours." This empowers the receiver to keep their responses to their working hours and not before or after hours.

Establishing clear priorities about what you will and will not do is key to integrating work and life. Though it's important to stay flexible, having a clear understanding of your non-negotiables empowers you to live both realms to the fullest.

---

[47] "Stress in America: A nation in political turmoil," American Psychological Association, survey, October 2024, https://www.apa.org/news/press/releases/stress.

Throughout my working life, it has helped me to set specific boundaries around when I'd be at work and when I'd be at home, or when I'd answer email messages. Even though the lines sometimes blurred — I'd occasionally find myself working on my computer at 10 p.m., finishing a memo while sitting on the floor of my daughter's bedroom — the framework I established set guardrails. It was a system that, though imperfect, seemed to work for everyone.

The beauty of breaks and boundaries

I grew up in the era of believing I could do it all and have it all and, as it turned out, I didn't have to. I was fortunate to choose a husband who stood behind me when my career began to take off. But as professor and economist Corinne Low of The Wharton School at the University of Pennsylvania has written, that's not the case for everyone: "There is simply no way to juggle a 50- to 80-hour career with full-time housework and — for those of us who are mothers — parenting load," she wrote in "Having It All: What Data Tells Us About Women's Lives and Getting the Most Out of Yours," which offers insights for using an evidence-based framework to make good decisions about work-life balance.[48]

It's true that no one can be everywhere all at once. Life is always a balancing act, and you have to make tough choices. Decisions about when to prioritize work and when to prioritize family likely will be some of the hardest you'll ever make. You'll miss out on some things in your personal life. You'll miss out on some office parties and after-work drinks.

But you can still make it work. Here are a few suggestions from my experience that may prove helpful:

---

[48] Corinne Low, *Having It All: What Data Tells Us About Women's Lives and Getting the Most Out of Yours,* Flatiron Books, MacMillan Publishers, September 23, 2025, Kindle excerpt, https://us.macmillan.com/books/9781250369512/havingitall/.

1. **Become a master scheduler.** I'm not a routine person, but I consider myself "very scheduled." Over the years, I've formally blocked off time for both work and personal events — as well as time to think instead of do. This helps me keep my priorities straight. (See Chapter 10 for more scheduling ideas.)

2. **Take a strategic approach to your life.** No matter how busy or under-resourced you are, it's important to step out of your day-to-day routine and reflect on your life — both at work and at home. To achieve this, carve out regular time for strategic analysis: Wake up earlier than your family, sequester yourself on a lunch break or take a walk. Looking at things from a higher level could help you get out of the weeds and into a more strategic way of thinking. What's going right? What's not? What could you change to make things better? Are there shortcuts that could save you time? Is there anything you could delegate or outsource? Would a different role or company be a better fit? A fresh perspective could lead you to make better decisions for yourself and your loved ones.

3. **Take a break.** Of course, there may be times when you don't have anyone to lean on, or the challenges of balancing your career and personal life are just too much. For example, if you don't have adequate support, you may struggle with decisions about opportunities or promotions. In these instances, make choices based on the support you do have. If the timing isn't right for a big career move, it isn't right. Keep cultivating your support system and keep your eyes open for the next opportunity. Nothing is permanent. You may have more capacity to ramp up your career at a later time. (See Chapter 6 for more on "Family first".)

Making work and family life work

Work-life balance isn't just a concern for women. My friend and colleague Joe Capper, CEO of MIMEDX, is a father of three, often worried about spending enough individual time with each of his children. When his kids were younger, he made reading with his children a nighttime ritual. On the evenings when he was too tired to read, he'd make up stories instead. This simple act of presence created special moments with his kids, who still fondly remember those times now that they're adults.

My good friend Cathy Langham, CEO of Langham Logistics, found a different approach. When her son was born, her mother-in-law commented, "I assume you're quitting work now that you have a baby." But as a business owner, Cathy didn't have that option, and she realized not everyone would support her choices. This fueled her determination to find a solution that worked for her family. As an entrepreneur, she had the flexibility to bring her son, Stephen, to work with her. She would take him to meetings in his car seat, where colleagues and customers were delighted to hold him. Soon, Stephen even had his own business card with his photo on it, blending family life with her career in a memorable, creative way. Eventually, Stephen was old enough to go to school, but he'd still come to work with his mom when he could. Today Stephen is a hard-working, business-savvy young man who still remembers going to work with his mom.

One of my top priorities has always been ensuring quality time with my family. Before I retired, this meant turning down evening events, dinners and cocktail parties that could cut into precious family moments. Networking in business often occurs over dinner and drinks and, as one of the few women in those circles, I had to devise a new approach. Instead of joining after-hours gatherings, I became the "lunch lady." Each day, I would invite colleagues — whether they were superiors, peers or team members — out for lunch. This not only became a platform for business discussions but also allowed me to connect, learn and enjoy a meal.

Building relationships at work

We often associate prioritizing our time with work-life balance — setting boundaries at work so we can have more time for family — but it's also important to have fulfilling relationships at your job.

Research supports the idea that building relationships is essential for success. A study noted in Harvard Business Review found that the strongest predictor of career advancement is not only hard work but also the depth of professional relationships.[49]

It's important to have allies and friends at every level — above, below and alongside you. The right connections can make your job more enjoyable and help you move forward in your career. If you don't have co-workers you'd actually want to grab lunch or coffee with, it might be worth rethinking your role — or even your company.

---

[49] Lauren Landry, "Why emotional intelligence is important in leadership," Harvard Business School Online, April 3, 2019, https://online.hbs.edu/blog/post/emotional-intelligence-in-leadership#:~:text=More%20than%20a%20decade%20ago%2C%20Goleman%20highlighted,come%20to%20be%20known%20as%20emotional%20intelligence.

TIFFANY'S TAKEAWAYS

- **Create boundaries — and refuse to compromise.** One of my essential rules is to clearly define where I refuse to make compromises. For example, I intentionally set aside time for exercise and family, and I commit to stop working at a specific hour. This approach was especially important when I had young children.

- **Establish your non-negotiable rules.** Identify whatever is necessary for you to maintain health and balance. Write down your non-negotiable rules on a piece of paper and put it where you'll regularly see it. Commit to making these rules principles you'll stand by without exception.

- **Reward yourself for holding firm.** The first time you uphold one of your rules or boundaries, celebrate. You'll feel empowered and energized. Remember that feeling as tasks and stress pile up during the day. By holding firm to your boundaries, you'll find greater fulfillment in both your personal and professional lives, leading to a more balanced, rewarding existence.

- **Use prioritization tools.** Practice using the WIN approach or the Eisenhower Matrix. These tools apply to both home and work. Reflect on how they could help you prioritize what's most important to you.

> ♦ **Take strategic breaks.** Regardless of the stage of your career, and no matter how busy or under-resourced you are, you owe it to yourself to step away from your day-to-day routine to gain perspective on your life. Grab time when you can to get out of the weeds and approach your life strategically. What's going well? What's not? What could you change to make things better.

Chapter 9

Overcome Imposter Syndrome and Share Your Authentic Story

Vulnerability fosters connection.

Imposter syndrome has a way of creeping in just when you're stepping into more responsibility. You start questioning whether you really have what it takes — whether you're good enough. When people struggle with feelings of unworthiness, they may hesitate to speak up or share personal experiences, believing that their voice lacks value or legitimacy. This internalized self-doubt can prevent people from embracing and expressing their true narratives, even when those stories are shaped by resilience and insight gained from years of hard-won experience. The irony is that the very act of storytelling — especially when it's raw and personal — can be one of the most powerful tools in dismantling imposter syndrome.

Sharing your authentic story is a bold declaration of self-acceptance. When you share your story, not as a resume of wins but as a real account of your journey, it builds trust. It gives others permission to be honest, too. And the act of owning your path — flaws, doubts, growth and all — is one of the most powerful ways to silence the voice calling you an imposter. Real leadership isn't about pretending to have all of the answers. It's about showing up with integrity and making space for others to do the same.

Imposter syndrome: a silent struggle among high achievers

It was an ordinary day in November in Indiana, which meant gray and dreary, when the unexpected happened. The global CEO of Roche asked me to meet him in the conference room. Instantly, my mind raced: Did I do something wrong? Had someone seen me sneak off to my child's soccer game? My numbers were just average that month — surely, they'd noticed.

This knee-jerk reaction was rooted in imposter syndrome, a phenomenon that affects countless high-achieving individuals. No matter how successful you are, there's often that nagging voice whispering doubts — "Am I really qualified for this?"

Here's an anecdote that helps illustrate the concept: At a prestigious university, a professor once addressed incoming freshmen, stating, "As you know, we have the highest standards for entry. However, sometimes a few people sneak through. Raise your hand if you feel you were one of those." Over a third of the students raised their hands. This shared vulnerability reveals that we're not alone in our doubts.

As I sat across from the CEO, I braced for the worst, ready to apologize for my perceived shortcomings. Instead, he asked if I'd consider a new position, relocating to Basel, Switzerland, that he believed would be the perfect fit for me, aimed at tackling some of the company's recent challenges. Relief washed over me; my doubts evaporated. This experience taught me that external validation is less impactful than internal belief. To combat imposter syndrome, it's crucial to build self-confidence from within.

Power poses: bodies building confidence

With more than 75 million views, Amy Cuddy's TED Talk about power posing and how to build confidence really resonates with me.[50] Before something important — an interview, a speech, an important meeting — I stand for two minutes with my hands on my hips like Wonder Woman. I adopt this power pose to align my body and mind and foster confidence.

Cuddy, an American social psychologist, researcher, bestselling author and keynote speaker, explains how animals in the wild expand their bodies to appear more powerful. Think of a peacock fanning its feathers or a gorilla pounding its chest. In contrast, when we feel nervous, we tend to shrink, crossing our legs or folding our arms.

During our meeting, I told the CEO that I needed to discuss the opportunity with my family. I walked out of the room, lifted my hands in the air and tilted my head back in a power pose. I didn't know then that it would have been better to strike a power pose before entering the room!

Building confidence by embracing challenges

That night, over pizza, everyone in my family — my husband, Brad, and our kids, Jess and Kevin — weighed in on the decision. Involving children in these discussions, even at a young age, can demystify the process of change and help them understand the uncertainties of life. Jess was excited about the prospect of learning German, while Kevin expressed concern about leaving his friends. Since Brad was all in and encouraged me to take the job, we ultimately decided to embrace the adventure together. That single decision opened up a world of experiences that shaped our family dynamics and individual identities.

---

[50] Amy Cuddy. "Power Poses," Pop!Tech conference, November 2, 2011, YouTube, 17 min., 24 sec., https://www.youtube.com/watch?v=phcDQ0H_LnY.

Moving to Switzerland was not just a geographical shift; it fundamentally transformed our lives. My daughter now speaks several languages fluently, and my son has adventures around the globe, climbing mountains and diving with sharks. This change instilled resilience and adaptability in my kids early on and it has served them well in adulthood. Brad adjusted quickly, too. He became a "hausmann," or a stay-at-home dad, and started meeting with a group of men who called themselves The Hausmen at an Irish pub. They watched American football while the kids talked and played in a cozy corner. As a family, we learned that change isn't to be feared but embraced.

Switzerland, with its four national languages and rich culture, presented challenges, but we prepared by taking German lessons. Jess excelled, while the rest of us struggled to learn basic phrases like, "How do I find the train station?" When we arrived in Basel, I began my role as global head of market development, quality and regulatory affairs, while my kids adjusted to their new international school and Brad managed things on the home front. When you live in a country where you don't speak the language, everything is hard to do.

I was going to be one of the few working women with young children on the team, and I'm an overly friendly American from the Midwest. Let's just say, I stood out.

While people were nice to me, there was a lack of connection. My colleagues were cordial in a polite, distant manner. I tried all of the tricks up my sleeve but felt like I was oversharing or that they weren't interested. With my imposter syndrome feelings, I needed to find something that built up my self-confidence and provided a connection to the people I was working with.

Bringing the walls down

Everything changed one fateful weekend. Brad, Jess, Kevin and our black Labrador retriever, Dakota, were all hanging out on the fourth floor of our apartment playing Chutes and Ladders. Suddenly, Dakota saw a bird. Outside. She started to run for it and before we knew it, she had leapt over the balcony — from the fourth floor. We all started screaming and ran over to the railing. We each peered over, afraid of what we would see. To our surprise, Dakota had somehow landed on a very small overhang only 3 feet wide by 6 feet long. The only problem was that it was 12 feet down from our balcony. She gave us a look that said, "How are you going to get me out of this mess?"

As if we were playing Chutes and Ladders in real life, the Olson family went into emergency survival mode. Brad leaned over the balcony; I held on to him and the kids grabbed my legs. Brad grabbed the scuff of Dakota's neck and launched our 100-pound lab back onto our balcony. We were all in shock but felt thankful that, besides being scared and a little scraped, Dakota was fine. We did a big family hug with Dakota in the middle.

When I returned to work on Monday, I decided to share the story of Dakota's daring leap. Instead of the typical, "Fine. How was your weekend?", I opened up about our wild adventure. To my surprise, sharing this authentic story sparked genuine interest. Colleagues began sharing their own pet stories and gradually the walls began to come down. I realized that vulnerability fosters connection; people respond to authenticity.

In Switzerland, I felt like I was doing everything in my job for the first time, despite my experience. People worked differently; I had to lead differently. I had to adapt my leadership style. To do that, I'd have to gather information and interpret it all through a new lens. It didn't happen overnight or over a weekend, but over the next several weeks, I built my self-confidence through connecting with others. Eventually, I felt like I belonged.

Connecting across cultures

A leadership style that works in Switzerland may not work in the United States. One of my favorite books on learning about how to do business in other countries is "The Culture Map: Breaking Through the Invisible Boundaries of Global Business" by Erin Meyer.[51]

The author includes research from more than 30 different countries and provides great insights. How can you learn to understand and read cultural nuances and adjust your approach accordingly? It takes time. It's good to observe and good to ask questions, but it's not good to make assumptions. Most people are happy to explain things if you ask with deep curiosity and respect. Acknowledging these differences fosters collaboration and ensures that teams operate cohesively, regardless of their backgrounds.

Storytelling as a leadership tool

Research has shown that storytelling is a powerful tool for leaders. It both humanizes leaders and builds trust and rapport. According to research published in the Harvard Business Review, stories can significantly increase engagement and retention of information.[52]

---

[51] Erin Meyer, *The Culture Map: Breaking Through the Invisible Boundaries of Global Business* (PublicAffairs, 2014), https://erinmeyer.com/books/the-culture-map/.
[52] Vanessa Boris and Lani Peterson, "What Makes Storytelling So Effective for Learning?" Harvard Business Impact Enterprise, accessed September 14, 2025, https://www.harvardbusiness.org/what-makes-storytelling-so-effective-for-learning/#:~:text=Good%20stories%20do%20more%20than,Better%20Business%20Connection"%2C%20wrote.

When we tell personal stories, we engage the listener emotionally, creating a shared experience that transcends the mere transmission of facts.

The connection I found through storytelling propelled me to a different level of leadership. Authenticity became my guiding principle. I learned that sharing stories creates opportunities for deeper engagement, empathy and trust within teams. We're inherently wired to connect through stories; they serve as vehicles for understanding values and culture, shaping our collective moral compass. In the corporate world, storytelling can be the linchpin of effective communication.

Crafting a compelling narrative requires mastering the mechanics of storytelling — developing an intriguing hook, relatable characters and a narrative arc filled with suspense, conflict and resolution. This is equally true in a business context. Capturing your audience's attention from the outset is vital. "Why should I listen to you?" is a question every speaker should anticipate. It's essential to clearly articulate the value of your message.

"You couldn't make it up!"

My good friend Cathy Langham, CEO of Langham Logistics, believes that reality is often far more exciting than anything she could have ever dreamed. She believes in telling authentic, real-life stories to engage her employees. Her favorite story started with what she thought was a crank call.

One day, her phone rang, and the caller ID read, "The White House." The person on the line said, "The president is going to be in town and wants to tour a local business."

Cathy was dumbfounded, but eventually she determined that the White House was, indeed, calling. The spokesperson for President George W. Bush wanted a virtual tour of her company and asked a lot of detailed questions, including a request that Cathy share her company's financial information.

Two days later, her White House contact called back and said, "President Bush will be there a week from tomorrow."

Cathy immediately gathered all of her employees to share the news, from office staff to drivers and warehouse workers. Some employees were clean cut; some had piercings and tattoos — the whole beautiful range of real people. Their reaction? They stared blankly, not sure how to react. So, she said, "You don't have to be here. We'll pay you to take the day off if you want." To her surprise, nearly all of them came and most brought their mothers!

It turned into a day that was bigger than the visit. Cathy introduced the president of the United States on live TV, receiving more than $4 million worth of media coverage. But the real story wasn't about the earned media or the cameras — it was about the people, the company's journey and how something so unbelievable became so personal.

That's why Cathy believes so strongly in sharing real stories — not just polished narratives, but messy, surprising, truly human stories. Because when we share authentically, we give others a glimpse of what's possible — not just in dreams, but in real life. And often, reality is far more effective than we ever imagined.

Practice makes perfect

I used to dread public speaking but also understood its importance for effective leadership. I attended seminars, took courses and even hired a coach.

I also practiced every chance I could. Toastmasters International, a global network of members that meet to learn public speaking, is a fantastic resource for honing these abilities. If a local club isn't accessible, recording yourself on your smartphone and then watching your performance can provide valuable feedback. Yes, at first it can be painful to see yourself onscreen, but it's an effective way to assess content and delivery and whether your message resonates.

One of the most transformative lessons I learned as a public speaker was to showcase my individuality. Authentic leadership means being true to yourself and allowing your personality to shine through.

My breakthrough moment came at a national sales meeting for Roche. The creative team tasked me with delivering a memorable, personal presentation that was light-hearted yet impactful, all in 15 minutes and right after lunch. Nervously, I chose to share the story about my Janesville moment (see Chapter 5), knowing it had the potential to resonate.

But there was a catch: I could use no notes or teleprompter. Just me and the audience of 500. My anxiety spiked as I walked on stage, fearing I'd trip or forget my speech. Just before my turn, a supportive team member reassured me, "I believe in you. If you get scared, just look at me; I've got your back."

As I began my story, I focused on him in the crowd. His encouragement gave me the confidence I needed to navigate the presentation. Each time I glanced at him, I felt more at ease. He helped me to have confidence and put my feelings of imposter syndrome behind. Today when I speak, I look for a friendly face in the audience. When others are presenting, I make sure they know they can look to me for support. It's a simple but supportive way to encourage one another.

TIFFANY'S TAKEAWAYS

- ◆ **Embrace the power of storytelling.** Stories connect us. They serve as a guide to values and culture. They reveal our moral compass and leave a lasting impact. Telling stories and sharing them is what makes us human. Stories are how we learn about each other and the world around us. In the business world, storytelling is the best way to make sure your audience understands and empathizes with you and your message. Stories help people remember and inspire them to take action.

- ◆ **Forge genuine connections.** The ability to connect, inspire and engage others is a hallmark of great leadership. You'll forge connections that lead to deeper relationships, stronger teams and more effective leadership. You could even propel your career to new heights.

- ◆ **Fake it till you make it.** Learning how to have confidence in what you're doing fosters more confidence in what you do. Next time you're feeling less than worthy, channel social psychologist Amy Cuddy and strike a power pose.

- ◆ **Share authentic stories.** Part of your job as a leader is to inspire people — and there's no better way to do that than to share stories that help people feel, think or do something differently. Embrace the power and authenticity of storytelling and never underestimate the impact of your story. Try these simple steps to prepare a story for your next team meeting.

1. Begin by reflecting on why you chose to join (or start) your company. What makes you proud to work there? Why do you continue to stay?
2. Next, think of a personal experience that illustrates why your job is meaningful to you. For instance, you might value the team environment because of your background in sports or appreciate the family-like atmosphere because you come from a large, close-knit family.
3. Once you have your story, share it with someone to get feedback, then refine it down to two minutes or less. Be succinct. Now you're ready to share your story with your team!

Chapter 10

Listen, Learn and Lead

Clear communication turns intention into action.

Genuinely listening to your team and learning from them is the foundation for effective leadership. When you tune in to the voices around you, rather than letting your mind race to the next thing you're going to say, you build trust, uncover new perspectives and create space for growth. Real leadership isn't about having all of the answers. It's about staying open, observing and adapting. From there, you can lead from an empowered place, but only if you do so out loud. Leaders must communicate their vision clearly, in a way that inspires and aligns a team. Clear communication, grounded in mutual respect and shared understanding, turns collaboration into momentum and intention into action.

A method that works in any workplace

Sometimes there are plans and sometimes there are opportunities. The plans are there to create opportunities, so that when one comes your way, you can be ready to grab it. This happened as soon as I'd made the big move to Switzerland with my family and started to get settled. The kids were happy in school, and I was finding my rhythm with the team. Then one day, I was unexpectedly called into my boss' office. Sitting across the desk, I was asked if I wanted to be the CEO of Roche Diagnostics Corporation back in the United States. In that moment, there was only one answer — yes.

I'd learned during my time in Basel that even though I was working for the same company, the way I worked had to be different. Whether you work on the frontline or in a support function, work in a large group or a small one, you'll still need to convince others to buy into your ideas. Keeping my leadership style flexible in different situations was essential to being successful.

I needed to return to Indiana a month before the kids were finished with school in Switzerland. My husband, Brad, stayed with the kids, and I started my new job as CEO of Roche Diagnostics Corporation. Every evening at 6 p.m. their time, 1 p.m. my time, I'd lock myself in my office, hang up a "do not disturb" sign and read Nancy Drew mysteries to my kids. I'd blocked off the time and told everyone "I had a meeting." It was the most important meeting of my day. That hour energized me, reconnected me to my family and enabled me to focus on my job. It also gave Brad a well-deserved break. I knew it was exactly what I needed to stay connected to my family and energized at work.

I still follow this practice. If I need focus time, I'll block one to two hours every morning to work on what I need to get done. Instead of making a to-do list, I've found it's good to block off time for things you need to get done on your calendar. The beauty of blocking off time is that you can say goodbye to endless lists and give yourself the time to actually get the stuff done. I know if it's on my calendar, I'll do it. In very stressful times, I sometimes even schedule daily reminders to take a deep breath.

I have a friend and former colleague who carves out 30 minutes each morning to sit quietly, drink coffee and watch the sunrise. She began with just three minutes a day and gradually worked up to half an hour. This dedicated time for herself not only improved her mental well-being but also set a positive tone for the rest of her day.

What stresses you? Learn the difference between good stress, called eustress, and bad stress, which is distress. Good stress energizes and excites us. It's what you feel before delivering a crucial presentation, reaching a personal milestone or facing a new challenge. This kind of stress drives us, invigorates us and helps us accomplish our objectives.

Bad stress, or distress, can be overwhelming and detrimental. It's the ongoing sensation of being swamped, unable to cope or constantly under strain. This is what most people are dealing with and why setting clear boundaries and specific focus time can help. Set small goals that are reachable when dealing with bad stress and reach out to others. Most likely they've experienced the same feelings and can provide tips on how to relieve the distress you're feeling.

My approach to leadership has always been to have regular, one-on-one meetings with everyone on my team. In this job, though, I had 4,000 employees and couldn't do one-on-ones. I needed to figure out how to scale up my leadership style.

It became evident to me right away that "what got you here won't get you there." The leadership approach that had served me well previously wouldn't necessarily guarantee success now.

"Just ask" had gotten me far, but I followed a new set of principles: Listen. Learn. Lead. I soon realized that it was the same technique I'd been using since I was a little girl playing store.

Plans are vital, but they must be flexible enough to allow for unexpected opportunities. Throughout my journey, I've learned that effective leadership is about listening deeply, committing to lifelong learning and articulating a clear vision.

LISTEN

Active listening is the first pillar of my scaled-up management technique and it's essential. Listen to people — internal team members, external contacts and peers in the industry — regardless of their title or rank. Pay attention not only to what's being voiced but also to what remains unspoken. It's in the silence that you discover the true dynamics within the organization. This type of listening can foster a culture of trust and uncover both obstacles and opportunities. When you prioritize absorbing information over immediately reacting, you'll be surprised by the insights you gain.

Effective listening starts with gentle probing. I always kick off discussions with a set of important-but-simple questions: What's wrong? What's right? What can we let go of? What are you willing to fight for? These questions usually get the conversation going. While listening, I remind myself not to defend the status quo or be defensive.

Other questions I've used are: If there were no limits on budget or resources, what would we do? What sets us apart in our industry? How do we eliminate bureaucracy? What's the fastest way of getting this done? What's the best way?

There are millions of questions you can ask depending on what you're trying to find out. Ensure the questions you ask are open-ended, inviting more than just a "yes" or "no" response, and then simply listen. Be sure the information you gain is only used in an aggregate, and there is no retaliation for the information anyone shares with you. Trust is hard to gain but very easy to lose.

LEGO listens

In 2012, The LEGO Group faced a significant decline in sales and relevance, particularly among older children and teenagers who were shifting toward digital entertainment. To turn the tide, the company initiated a groundbreaking approach by embracing feedback from both customers and employees.

Instead of relying solely on internal ideas, LEGO launched a platform called LEGO Ideas. This initiative encouraged fans to submit their own designs for new LEGO sets. The company committed to reviewing each submission and promised to produce sets based on popular ideas. This move not only opened up the creative process but also allowed LEGO to directly engage with its passionate fanbase.

One notable success story was the Women of NASA set, proposed by a fan who aimed to celebrate the contributions of women in the space industry. The idea garnered significant support, and LEGO recognized the importance of highlighting diversity and representation. The final product included mini figures of astronauts like Mae Jemison and Sally Ride, resonating with both young builders and adult fans.[53]

By listening to customers and valuing their input, LEGO was able to innovate successfully. Sales surged and the brand became synonymous with creativity and inclusivity.

Safety in sharing, success in teamwork

In the electric utility industry, there are few events more devastating than an ice storm. When one of the worst storms in years was expected to hit Indianapolis, my good friend Ann Murtlow, who at the time was president, CEO and director of Indianapolis Power & Light (now AES Indiana), knew

---

[53] Epi Ludvik, "Women of NASA Creator to Inspire New Generation with LEGO toys," Crowd Sourcing Week, accessed April 25, 2025, https://crowdsourcingweek.com/blog/woman-nasa-creator-maia-weinstock-lego-ideas.

that her team, while prepared, needed to be deeply aligned in real time to get the best results for customers.

Keeping the power on for hundreds of thousands of households and businesses while ensuring that employees stayed safe was the goal. In order for the leadership team to perform at their best, they had to be together in one place, trust each other and communicate effectively. Ann made sure that there was an environment where everyone could bring their unique thoughts and ideas to the team and that she and everyone else on the team would listen. It was a safe environment for her leadership team to share real-time information, challenge each other and quickly agree on a course of action that all could wholeheartedly support. Thankfully, the storm wasn't as bad as originally feared, but the team achieved excellence in storm response through seamless teamwork, mutual respect and a bias to action.

Remember that your job is not to have all of the answers. Your job is to ask the right questions of the right people, then listen. By incorporating ideas and insights from others, you'll achieve the best possible outcome. When people feel listened to and valued, remarkable changes can occur throughout the entire company.

LEARN

Next, prepare yourself to embrace learning. Be willing to get dusty. This concept goes beyond merely walking in someone else's shoes; it involves trailing behind others, becoming enveloped in their dust and absorbing their knowledge. In ancient times, when a rabbi invited a new disciple with the words, "Follow me," it signified a commitment to closely observe and learn from the rabbi's teachings. As the disciple departed, others would express the wish, "May you be covered with the dust of your rabbi," reminding the disciple to become immersed in learning.[54]

Collecting information and learning can be done in many different ways. Have lunch with an expert, someone outside of your industry dealing with the same type of challenges. Use studies, past presentations and industry information and look for themes. Pay attention to what your own organization and its employees are teaching you. Consider what you've heard, what you've learned (your dusty experience) and all of the data points you've collected along the way.

Now, it's time to make sense of everything you've gathered. Look for patterns or commonalities in the information you've received. Identify themes that consistently emerge. Do you have sufficient insight to delineate the strengths and weaknesses of the situation? Can you distill the key messages into three to five bullet points? Once you have it crystal clear, you can run with it. And others will run with you; that's called leadership.

LEAD

Now you're ready to lead. Be sure to do it out loud!

Leading out loud means speaking up and helping everyone understand your values, mission, vision, strategy and goals. Be transparent and keep talking.

Think of this next phase as your leadership tour. You'll need to articulate your message, then repeat it ... and repeat it. By the time you're absolutely sick of talking about it, it may just be getting through to the people in your organization. Repetition allows people to hear the message, understand it and take action. The rule of seven in marketing refers to the idea that it takes,

---

[54] Mishnah, *Pirkei Avot* 1:4.

on average, seven messages to a customer before they make a purchase. Think of commercials and how and why they're successful.[55]

I've applied this method to other areas of my life. For example, at my house I often have to ask repeatedly before someone in my family takes action. "Can you please take out the garbage?" "Can someone take out the garbage?" "Is that garbage in the kitchen?" "You're going outside? The garbage!" "Can you take out the f------ garbage?!" You get the picture; it takes repetition, and you'll need to repeat your vision for everyone to hear and act on the message.

Constant and effective communication demands that you explain your vision and goals and how they directly affect both employees and customers on a personal level. If you don't share the direction of the business, others won't know and that leaves room for negative assumptions to fill the void. A leader's job is to calm the chaos, not create it.

Explaining the path forward by painting a clear picture of the destination ahead will ease uncertainties and free your team to focus on what's most important.

Defining your vision

If you want people to focus on your mission and strategy, they need to understand those concepts well enough to articulate them. If your strategy is too long, they won't remember it, but if they can say it in less than two minutes, they'll remember it and find themselves in it. To facilitate understanding, create clear definitions that every employee can understand. This chart highlights easy-to-understand definitions of mission, vision, values, strategy and goal that have helped my teams in the past:

---

[55] Indeed Editorial Team, "The Marketing Rule of 7: Tips for Using It To Convert Leads, Indeed, July 26, 2025, https://www.indeed.com/career-advice/career-development/rule-of-7-marketing.

MISSION	VISION	VALUES	STRATEGY	GOAL
Today	One day	Every day	How you put mission, vision and values to work	A milestone to measure progress
This is your purpose — what you do **right now**.	This is where you're going in the **future** — what you hope to achieve. Your vision should be inspiring.	This is where the culture really shines. Values are not changeable or negotiable.	Strategy is the **single most important thing** you need to act upon to achieve your vision. Create a one-year, five-year and 10-year plan.	Your metric could be gaining market share, reaching a sales target or growing faster than the market.

Recently I had an opportunity to connect with a former employee. He said, "I don't like where I am now because there's no focus. We're always chasing the shiny new object. The priority changes monthly and it feels like we never get anywhere. We just spin. I miss your leadership because you always told us what was important and where we needed to focus our energy." This affirmation reminded me to keep communicating out loud — and keep leading out loud.

Leading out loud is relatively easy for me; I'm an extrovert. But my leadership teams have frequently included introverts. To help more-reserved team members thrive, I'd give them time to process topics, inform them in advance when they'd need to present and support them in developing their ability to lead out loud. Even if it was out of their comfort zone to speak out, it was essential for them to communicate their thoughts and expectations clearly to their teams — because leadership isn't just about making decisions; it's about sharing them. Authentic leadership means embracing your own style, but even as an introvert, practicing speaking to both large and small groups can significantly expand your influence. Be sure you lead — out loud — every day.

TIFFANY'S TAKEAWAYS

- 💎 **Lead from where you are.** No matter your position in an organization, you have the power to lead. Leadership isn't about titles — it's about taking action from where you are. Don't assume that the CEO, the board or even your manager knows about an issue or will address it; they may not even be aware of it. This is your opportunity to step up: Listen, learn and lead from wherever you are.

- 💎 **Listen actively.** Begin by listening to the challenges your colleagues or customers are facing. Watch for both verbal and nonverbal cues. Ask probing questions that help you discover the truth about what people think and how they feel.

- 💎 **Make your mission, vision and values clear.** If you want people to focus on your mission and strategy, they need to understand those concepts well enough to articulate them. If your strategy is too long, they won't remember it, but if they can say it in less than two minutes, they'll remember it and find themselves in it. Create clear definitions of the words mission, vision, values, strategy and goal and what they mean to your organization. Make sure every employee understands these terms.

- 💎 **Explore solutions collaboratively.** You may need to solicit other teammates' help in problem-solving. This approach involves others in the solution, which is empowering for everyone and enhances buy-in.

◆ **Champion your ideas.** Next, lead by sharing your ideas with your manager and others, highlighting the positive impact your solution could bring. This is guaranteed to get you noticed in the best possible way.

CHAPTER 11

Don't Be Afraid to Be Vulnerable

When you allow yourself to be real, you create deeper connections with those around you.

Vulnerability is often seen as a weakness, but in leadership, it's a powerful strength. When you allow yourself to be real — owning your uncertainties, mistakes and emotions and asking for help when you need it — you create deeper connections with those around you. This kind of authenticity builds trust and encourages others to show up fully, too. Vulnerability strips away the noise and ego, helping you get clear on what truly matters to you. In that honesty, you begin to uncover your "why" — the deeper purpose behind your actions and choices. Leading from that place of truth not only makes you more relatable; it makes you more resilient, intentional and impactful.

From providing to receiving: my story of raw vulnerability

I was in the middle of my life. Everything was going great. My family and I had been back from Switzerland for several years. My job as CEO of Roche Diagnostics Corporation was keeping me busy, and the business was doing well. I felt I was really hitting my stride, and all of my previous work was starting to pay off. I was in love with my husband, Brad and had a strong, happy marriage. Our two children, Jess and Kevin, were in seventh and eighth grade and doing well in school. They'd adjusted well coming back to the United States and were really blossoming. They had new friends, they loved the caring atmosphere at their new school, Park Tudor, and we were building a new home in Westfield. Brad got back to golfing, hunting and fishing, and I felt like we were really taking root in the community. Life was incredible, but I didn't know about the silent killer in my body.

One day, not long after I'd had my annual mammogram, my phone rang. My radiologist and friend, Dr. Gordon McLaughlin, was calling to ask me to stop by for lunch. I didn't think much of it at the time. But when Gordon met me at the door and walked me into his office, I knew something was up. My husband, Brad, was sitting at a conference table next to my file and a box of tissues. This is not good news, I thought. But I hadn't imagined how bad it would be.

Life-changing news

In a snap of my fingers, my life changed: I was diagnosed with breast cancer. Shortly after my diagnosis, my oncologist had this advice: "Get your affairs in order."

I got physically sick when he told me that. In a moment, I went from providing healthcare services at Roche Diagnostics to receiving healthcare services. And I discovered firsthand that providing healthcare services is a whole lot better than receiving them.

As I went through the phases of my treatment — chemotherapy, radiation and surgery, my relationships changed. My doctor had warned me that cancer is not a one-person disease. When one member of the family has cancer, the whole family is affected. I found this to be true. The people in my family, as well as my close friends, were shaken by the news. For years, I'd played the part of the strong advocate who loved ones could lean on, talk to about their troubles and ask for advice. All of a sudden, the conversations were about how I was feeling. And, more disturbing, if I was going to make it.

After my treatments began, there were many days when I just couldn't get out of bed. The vomiting, body aches and depression were just too great. Brad picked up the slack at home. He accompanied me to medical appointments and started answering my phone, as the calls could drain the little energy that I had. I learned I had to rely on him, and others, in a whole new way — a more vulnerable way than ever before.

Throughout my chemo, radiation and surgeries, I never asked, "Why me?" I started to ask questions like, "Why anyone?"

"Would somebody please hold my hand?"

After I was diagnosed and before my treatment started, I had a biopsy. The doctor used a pen to mark the area of my body where cancerous tissue would be extracted, then sent to the laboratory for processing. For those not familiar with an MRI, it involves lying on a narrow table that slides into a tight tube. The machine was loud, and I was claustrophobic and scared. The only part of my body outside of the machine was my wrist. So I could be heard above the din of the machine, I shouted, "Please, would somebody hold my hand?"

One of the assistants held my hand and never let go for the entire 30-minute procedure. This was a lesson in kindness. I never would have received this kindness if I hadn't allowed myself to be vulnerable. I learned that when going through cancer treatment, sometimes you need to ask someone to hold your hand — even if it's a stranger. I thought about the second-grade teacher who gave me a hug when I arrived at school smelling like burnt toast and friends who had reached out with kindness. Providing kindness isn't hard. It's easy to do and can be just what a person needs. True kindness leaves a lasting impression.

Dr. Connie Harrill, the physician who did the biopsy that day, eventually became a close friend. She introduced me to another woman who had breast cancer and the three of us became a support group. Seventeen years later, we're still supporting each other.

Health equity and cancer: purpose through vulnerability

My first chemo treatment taught me that cancer doesn't discriminate. As I walked into a big room with infusion chairs all around it, I noticed all types of people — old and young; white, Black, Asian and Hispanic; affluent and poor; sophisticated and not so sophisticated.

One in eight women in the United States are diagnosed with breast cancer each year.[56] Being one of them made me want to take my fight against the disease to a higher level. The voice in my head grew louder. "Why does anyone have to go through this?" I thought. "What can we do to prevent and cure cancer for everyone?"

As my cancer journey continued, I realized that the answer to the question "Why anyone?" always comes back to research. The intersection of funding and research is where we'll find a cure and that cure needs to be for everyone. Cancer doesn't care about your background. That's why

---

[56] American Cancer Society, Breast Cancer Facts & Figures 2024-25, 1, https://www.cancer.org/content/dam/cancer-org/research/cancer-facts-and-statistics/breast-cancer-facts-and-figures/2024/breast-cancer-facts-and-figures-2024.pdf.

health equity — good healthcare for everyone — is so important. We can't discriminate, especially in research.

I'm not a doctor or scientist, but I have a knack for giving a voice to science. When I switched roles from provider to receiver of healthcare, I became intimately involved in how the system worked, and my background in the life sciences helped me identify where the gaps were.

Often researchers struggle with securing funding, samples and patients for clinical studies. I knew what I had to do: Become an activist for research — specifically in helping to find funding and making it easier for researchers to access human samples.

My mission became clear. But I couldn't have imagined how well it would dovetail with pro football's showpiece event.

A game-changing project

In 2012, Indianapolis was home to Super Bowl XLVI. The excitement in the city reached a fever pitch as everyone prepared for the New York Giants to battle the New England Patriots. I got excited about a different battle: Indy's Super Cure versus breast cancer.

When a city hosts the Super Bowl, it's a great opportunity to funnel energy into community projects, and I'd just joined an amazing group of women with a game-changing project in mind.

The Indy's Super Cure initiative was born to raise awareness, provide education and secure donations of both money and healthy breast tissue to fight cancer. The program was the brainchild of Allison Melangton, who at the time served as president and CEO of the 2012 Indianapolis Super Bowl Host Committee. Allison and her team were responsible for everything about the event except the actual football game.

I co-chaired Indy's Super Cure with my good friend and fellow cancer survivor Cathy Langham. The impact of our efforts would be both local and global. Indianapolis is home to the world's only healthy breast tissue bank: the Susan G. Komen Tissue Bank at Indiana University Melvin and Bren Simon Comprehensive Cancer Center.

Cathy and I gathered over 100 passionate volunteers and aligned on a mission. We had two key priorities: first, to increase minority participation among healthy breast tissue donors, and second, to reach a $1 million fundraising goal for the healthy breast tissue bank.

We raised awareness by gaining airtime during the Super Bowl pregame show and through several fundraising events. I'm proud to say we exceeded our goals: We helped raise over $2 million for breast cancer research and more than 1,000 women gave the greatest gift imaginable: a piece of themselves — tissue for research.[57]

Supporting women-led research

As a breast cancer survivor with a family history of the disease — my mom and maternal grandmother were both survivors — my passion is driven by the hope that my daughter and future generations of women may be spared from it. That is why finding a cure matters so deeply to me.

In 2019, I became involved with the ResearcHERS project, which was initiated by the American Cancer Society to support and sustain women-led cancer research.[58] Money raised through ResearcHERS funds top female cancer researchers who are spearheading critical studies in oncology.

---

[57] Newsroom, "Nearly 700 Women Donate to Indy's Super Cure Breast Tissue Collection Event," Indiana University School of Medicine, February 2, 2012, https://medicine.iu.edu/news/2012/02/nearly-700-women-donate-to-indys-super-cure-breast-tissue-collection-event.

[58] "ResearcHERS: Women Fighting Cancer," American Cancer Society, accessed September 17, 2025, https://secure.acsevents.org/site/SPageServer?pagename=researchers_home.

Since the inception of the project, I've donated to, worked on and co-chaired the regional ResearcHERS campaign in Indiana.

Making our mess our message

When I first opened up about my cancer journey, I felt vulnerable and afraid. I worried that if people knew about my illness, I might seem weak or unfit for my job. But I was consistently amazed at how many people were touched or inspired by my story. Many people would approach me after I spoke about my cancer journey to share their own experiences with illness, revealing just how universal these health challenges are.

Talking about breast cancer gave me a way to explain my deep passion for healthcare, my commitment to raising funds for research and my dedication to educating others about cancer screening and resources. As I continued to share my story, I found strength as a leader and encouraged others to connect with and voice their own motivations for being engaged in finding a cure.

I'd become more than a survivor. To survive is to remain alive, to exist, to function. I became a thriver. Thriving is about growth, development and flourishing. My cancer journey, the worst thing that ever happened to me, became a vital part of my leadership legacy.

Robin Roberts, news anchor for ABC's "Good Morning America," had a similar experience. She was navigating her own cancer journey at the same time I was going through mine and the way she articulated her experience deeply resonated with me.

Roberts has said that she often recalls her mother's words: "Make your mess your message."[59] Roberts took it a step further and turned her "mess" into

---

[59] Robin Roberts, "Make Your Mess Your Message," Master Class, accessed April 25, 2025, https://www.masterclass.com/classes/robin-roberts-teaches-effective-and-authentic-communication/chapters/make-your-mess-your-message.

a platform, using her journey to speak for others facing similar struggles. The power of her story became particularly evident in 2012, when she was diagnosed with myelodysplastic syndrome (MDS), a bone marrow disease. After she shared her diagnosis publicly, and was preparing for a bone marrow transplant, Be The Match, a stem cell donor program, saw a huge spike in donor registrations.[60]

Roberts' willingness to be vulnerable had an extraordinary impact, reaching thousands of people she'd never even meet.

Stories of triumph: vulnerability to victory

Once is bad, twice is a curse, but three times takes a spirit that won't quit. My good friend Cathy Langham is a three-time cancer survivor.

Her senior year in high school, Cathy was diagnosed with Hodgkin's disease, now known as Hodgkin lymphoma. In the mid-1970s, there were few survivors of Hodgkin lymphoma — she would be one of the first. As she started her freshman year of college, Cathy realized that she needed more help and moved back home for treatments. This is when she made up her mind to live her life "all in." She eventually started her own successful business and years later would be inducted into the Indiana Business Hall of Fame. Right at the time she received this prestigious award, she received her second cancer diagnosis. This time it was breast cancer. After surgery, radiation and chemotherapy, Cathy was diagnosed again, five years later. What she learned through all of this was to never give up.

There will be all kinds of setbacks in your life — all kinds — but how you deal with them will set the course of your life. There is no better example of this than Olympic gymnast Simone Biles.

---

[60] "Making Memories with Robin Roberts: Our Top 10!" NMDP, formerly the National Marrow Donor Program and Be The Match, September 20, 2022, https://www.nmdp.org/what-we-do/news/press-releases/making-memories-with-robin-roberts.

Biles' 37 medals, including 11 Olympic medals and 30 World Championship medals, make her the most decorated gymnast in history,[61] and she's widely considered to be one of the greatest gymnasts of all time.

In the summer of 2021, Biles shocked the world by withdrawing from several events during the Tokyo Olympics. After dominating gymnastics for years, her decision to prioritize her mental health over competition was unprecedented. Biles had always been celebrated for her physical prowess, but this moment revealed a deeper aspect of her leadership: vulnerability and the courage to listen to her own needs.

Leading up to the Olympics, Biles experienced intense pressure, both from the expectations of winning and the relentless scrutiny of the media. When she began to feel the effects of "the twisties" — a term used in gymnastics to describe a loss of spatial awareness — she recognized that continuing to compete could jeopardize her safety. Rather than pushing through for the sake of medals, she chose to step back and focus on her mental well-being.

This decision was not just about her personal health; it sent a powerful message to athletes and leaders everywhere. Biles' act of prioritizing her own mental health challenged the stigma surrounding mental health in general, encouraging others to speak up about their struggles. She used her platform to advocate for the importance of mental wellness, demonstrating that true strength lies in acknowledging when you need help.

Biles also highlighted the importance of a supportive environment. Throughout her career, she has credited her coaches and teammates for creating a space where she could express her vulnerabilities. This atmosphere of trust and open communication enabled her to take the necessary steps for her

---

[61] "Simone Biles: All titles, records and medals — complete list," International Olympic Committee, accessed September 14, 2025, https://www.olympics.com/en/news/simone-biles-all-titles-records-medals-complete-list.

well-being. By sharing her experience, she encouraged other athletes to listen to their bodies and minds, fostering a culture of empathy in sports.

In the aftermath of the Olympics, Biles became an even more impactful leader. She participated in discussions about mental health in sports, collaborating with organizations to raise awareness and promote resources for athletes facing similar challenges. Her story emphasizes that leadership is not solely about victories; it's about listening, learning and setting an example for others to prioritize their health.[62]

Simone Biles turned a potential setback into a profound opportunity for growth and leadership, both for herself and for the broader athletic community. By embracing vulnerability, she demonstrated that true leadership comes from understanding and supporting one another, ultimately inspiring countless individuals to value their mental health alongside their ambitions.

Reckoning and rumbling with Brené Brown

Brené Brown, a researcher who has studied courage and vulnerability for decades, has published several books that touch on this topic, ranging from vulnerability in interpersonal relationships to vulnerability in leadership. She challenges her audience to think of vulnerability, putting yourself out there without guarantees, as an act of courage.

"Vulnerability is not winning or losing," Brown has written. "It's having the courage to show up and be seen when we have no control over the outcome. Vulnerability is not weakness; it's our greatest measure of courage."[63]

---

[62] "Simone Biles: A Journey from Early Years to Sporting Glory," International Olympic Committee, accessed September 17, 2025, https://www.olympics.com/en/athletes/simone-biles.
[63] Brené Brown, *Rising Strong: The Reckoning. The Rumble. The Revolution.* (Random House, 2015).

In her book "Rising Strong: The Reckoning. The Rumble. The Revolution," Brown asserts that if you're brave with your life, failure is inevitable. But that's not the point. The point is what happens when you're in between failing and getting back up.

Remember the concept of resilience? That's what "Rising Strong" is all about — allowing your failures or setbacks to shape you for the better rather than break you.

Brown's rising strong process has three parts. During the "Reckoning" phase, you contend with your situation; instead of pushing it away or denying it, you get curious about it. During the "Rumble" phase, you confront the story you're telling yourself, examining if it's rooted in shame or fear. Here you confront your pain, motives and assumptions and seek the truth. This is where you grow. In the final phase, the "Revolution," you take the insights you've gleaned from your experience and move forward, stronger than ever, because you're emerging from an experience with clarity, honesty and in alignment with your values. It's during this phase that we choose courage over comfort because of the emphasis on values.

"When we deny our stories, they define us," Brown has said. "When we own our stories, we get to write the ending."[64] "Rising Strong" is a handbook for emotional resilience. I highly recommend it! Brown teaches that failure and struggle aren't signs we're broken — they're invitations to become whole. We don't have to pretend we're fine; we need to own our truth and stand up, again and again.

In her book "Dare to Lead," Brown brings these ideas to the workplace. She advocates for leaders stepping away from comfort and into courage by being vulnerable. If leaders can master this, it becomes a superpower. This ability

---

[64] Brené Brown, *How the Ability to Reset Transforms the Way We Live, Love, Parent and Lead* (Random House, 2017).

allows people to connect with them on a level where they can be inspired. It also creates trust in the workplace. Vulnerability is crucial for psychologically safe environments conducive to innovation and creativity. Leaders can create these environments, and therefore stronger teams, by admitting their mistakes, asking for help when they need it and modeling courage.[65]

Don't be afraid to be vulnerable. As a leader, you don't have to be fearless all of the time; you just have to have enough courage to be real. It's not an easy path, but it's one that leads to a deeper, richer life, both personally and professionally.

---

[65] Brené Brown, *Dare to Lead: Brave Work. Tough Conversations. Whole Hearts.* (Random House, 2019).

TIFFANY'S TAKEAWAYS

- ◆ **Seek purpose in times of adversity.** The news of my cancer diagnosis was devastating and the journey harrowing, but my experiences opened my eyes to what it's really like to be a cancer patient. I saw my profession in a new way and discovered a new mission. In the same way, your life's struggles hold the potential for personal growth and transformation. Facing and navigating difficulties can lead you to a deeper understanding of yourself and the world around you, fostering resilience and opening your eyes to new perspectives and goals.[66]

- ◆ **Be open to acts of kindness.** Welcome kindness, even from strangers, especially when you're feeling vulnerable. Experiencing acts of kindness produces the hormone oxytocin, which aids in lowering blood pressure and increases optimism and self-esteem.[67] It may even lead to rewarding new relationships.

- ◆ **Make your mess your message.** Use your personal challenges to help others understand who you are and what drives you. People will remember how you made them feel and this creates a lasting impact. Show others that overcoming adversity fuels your passion and determination. We've all faced obstacles that shook us, held us back or forced us to reset. By sharing your story, you form a lasting memory and connection with others.

---

[66] Paula Davis, "How Adversity Makes You Stronger," *Psychology Today*, April 9, 2020, https://www.psychologytoday.com/us/blog/pressure-proof/202004/how-adversity-makes-you-stronger.

[67] "The Science of Kindness," Random Acts of Kindness Foundation, accessed September 14, 2025, https://www.randomactsofkindness.org/the-science-of-kindness.

> ◆ **Own — and share — your stories.** Before meeting with your team, think about a challenge you've overcome. Consider the key points of the story and try to tell it in under three minutes. This will take time, repetition and practice. Then, share it with your team. Let them know why you're passionate about your role, your company or your project. You'll be amazed at how many people you'll touch and inspire.

Chapter 12

Pick the Right Strategy and Celebrate the Wins

Clear direction turns chaos into forward motion.

When you're guiding a team or building a business, you need more than ambition — you need a sound, adaptable strategy. Clear direction gives your team confidence. It aligns their efforts, filters out distractions and turns chaos into forward motion. Without it, even the most talented workers will eventually burn out chasing unclear goals.

But leadership doesn't end with structure. Acknowledging wins — big, small and especially early on — isn't fluff. It's fuel. It builds momentum, reinforces the right behaviors and reminds your team why the work matters. A culture that celebrates progress breeds loyalty, drive and resilience. It turns effort into pride and keeps standards high while keeping things in proportion. The best leaders balance both precise strategy and powerful recognition. That's how you build teams that win — and keep winning.

Recovered and ready for my next role

As I was recovering from my cancer treatments and hunkering down to build up physically and mentally, I was doing a lot of consulting in the field of diagnostics. I was pretty sure I didn't want to go back to working full time and traveling all over the world. I received an email message from a recruiter. He asked me if I'd be interested in applying for the position of president of a nuclear division at Cardinal Health. I wasn't sure if I wanted another big challenge. I wasn't sure if it would be the right move. But, as my mother always told me, don't judge first; find out more.

I had my first interview and really liked that the position would be relatively autonomous, and I'd have the freedom to be creative and innovative. When you're working in a big corporation, the advantage, of course, is the huge platform, lots of resources and instant brand recognition, but we all know there's often bureaucracy and tedious processes. What appealed to me about the position from the start — and what continued to appeal to me — was the freedom to move quickly, make decisions rapidly and have strong connections to my team.

I took the job. They told me during the interview process that the division was struggling, and right away I realized the challenges were in both the market and the business itself. We needed to do things differently.

A "market-in" strategy

Having the right strategy is the single most important aspect a business needs to be successful. It's something I can't stress enough: Always continue to work on your strategy. You'll need to act upon your strategy to achieve your vision, and you'll need a well-executed strategy to win. In the marketplace, winning is about understanding why your customers buy from you.

When I asked my team what our differentiation was in the market, they couldn't answer the question. To be an industry leader, you need differentiation and a value proposition, and we didn't have either. But before we developed those things, we needed to understand how our customers felt about us. (See Chapter 5: Put the Customer First.) We needed to understand what was important to our customers and how we were going to bring them value.

We needed a "market-in" strategy. This is a strategy that starts with going out to your customers and asking them about your services, how they rank you compared to your competition and why they buy (or don't buy) from you. We surveyed over 2,000 customers in a blind study and found out they knew who we were and they used our products, but they didn't see any difference between us and the competition. When this happens in the market, you become a commodity. It's all about price. This is never a place you want to be. Regardless of the industry, being the lowest-price provider is never sustainable. Someone can always have a lower price than you. You must differentiate with products or services to win.

Our problem was well defined. Our market had become commodity based, where low price was king. Our customers didn't have much to say about our product and services. As a matter of fact, when our customers told us what they wanted in our survey, they ranked price last. They were looking for value in services, but we'd assumed they wanted a lower price.

I gathered the team. We looked at the data and thought about what was missing from our current offerings. To gather ideas for how to differentiate our services, we reached out to a lot of people and asked "What crazy thing can we do next?"

The funnel method

We took everyone's ideas, looked at the survey data and started to put together a plan for how we could meaningfully differentiate our company. To pick the best ideas and provide focus for the organization, we used the funnel method to decide which ideas we should work on first, second and never.

The funnel method is a technique for ranking ideas based on a variety of parameters such as the number of people and the skill sets required, the cost of the project, the length of time needed, the profit upon completion and the degree of difficulty to succeed. We waited to see which ideas emerged from the bottom of the funnel. From there, we picked the top 10 ideas, formed pilot teams and started implementation.

Maintaining momentum

This was our new strategy — adding services and products that differentiated us from the competition. It was a long-term transition.

Guess what? Your strategy is only good if your internal team believes it's good. It's only as good as your ability to implement it, and it's only as good as your momentum to keep it going. That's why it's so important to celebrate as you go.

We celebrated successes — both big and small wins — along the way, and we made sure everyone in the organization understood our direction was the right one. Our celebrations gave people in the organization a chance to pause, reflect on their hard work, receive recognition and stay aligned.

After five years, we'd met all of our goals. We'd differentiated our products and services. Our profit quadrupled and revenue increased substantially. Our customers rewarded us with their loyalty and willingness to pay a premium over the competition.

Effective communication: a winning strategy

From a young age, my friend and colleague Joe Capper, CEO of MIMEDX, quickly learned that understanding people was the key to setting the right personal strategy. Starting with odd jobs at gas stations, landscaping and then working at 7-Eleven when he was 15, Joe picked up lessons about communication and patience. He saw firsthand how different people — whether struggling and using food stamps or flush with cash — needed to be approached differently. Small tweaks, like changing the phrase "Is that all?" to "Would you like something else?" made a big difference. It taught him that how you say things can shape relationships.

Joining the military reinforced and enhanced these lessons. Joe learned to make decisions quickly and effectively and to create clear plans for achieving his goals. Leading 60 people across different roles, he realized that good leadership strategy isn't about knowing everything — it's about listening, guiding and respecting others. The key was understanding people's needs and adapting accordingly.

Looking back, Joe sees that his most successful strategy was simply connecting with people and communicating with respect. Those early lessons stuck with him, showing him that sometimes, small adjustments and genuine understanding are the most powerful strategy tools for fostering success.

Choosing the right moment to act

When my friend and colleague Derek Maetzold, founder, president and CEO of Castle Biosciences, was in high school, he developed a smart strategy that stuck with him throughout his career. He worked a part-time sales job at Sears, selling service contracts for appliances. It wasn't a glamorous job, but it taught him one of his first lessons in strategy. The team faced pressure every week to hit sales numbers, especially toward the end of the week — managers would offer quick cash bonuses to whoever closed the most sales on Thursdays and Fridays.

Most representatives scrambled to make it happen, but instead of playing the game on their terms, Derek found a smarter approach. He'd often hit his quota early in the week — Monday or Tuesday. Rather than turning in all his sales right away, he'd hold a few back and time them to drop just when the incentives were hot. Same sales, same effort — just better timing.

Derek understood how the system worked and played it to his advantage. That simple shift made him the top performer, even beating out seasoned representatives twice his age.

The strategy takeaway? Sometimes success isn't about working harder — it's about choosing the right moment to act. To find the right moment, consider all of the angles: marketing campaigns, new product launches, seasonal changes and company needs and work within the framework to achieve the best possible outcome.

Strategy successes and failures in big business

When it comes to strategy, we've all witnessed examples of success and failure. I wrote in Chapter 7 about Netflix being at the forefront of taking risks. Well, while Netflix took risks, Blockbuster, the once-dominant video rental giant, disappeared because the company wasn't agile and responsive to the market's needs. At its peak in the late 1990s and early 2000s, Blockbuster had thousands of locations worldwide; it was synonymous with home entertainment. However, the company's failure to adapt to changing consumer habits ultimately led to its demise. As streaming services like Netflix began to rise in popularity, Blockbuster stuck to its brick-and-mortar model, prioritizing late fees and physical rentals over innovation. Although Blockbuster had the opportunity to purchase Netflix in its early days, the company's leadership dismissed the idea, believing that customers preferred the physical rental experience.[68]

---

[68] Frank Palmer, "Blockbuster Turned Down Chance to Buy Netflix in 2000," Screen Geek, May 4, 2024, https://www.screengeek.net/2024/05/04/blockbuster-turned-down-netflix/#:~:text=Blockbuster%20had%20a%20chance%20to,thinking%20it%20was%20too%20expensive.

By the time Blockbuster attempted to launch its own streaming service, it was too late: Customers had already transitioned to more convenient, on-demand options. Blockbuster declared bankruptcy in 2010, with only a single store remaining operational in 2023, serving as a poignant reminder of the importance of flexibility and foresight in business.

I love stories of crazy business ideas that only seem crazy until they disrupt the market. A remarkable success story is that of Airbnb, which started from a seemingly crazy idea. In 2007, founders Brian Chesky and Joe Gebbia were struggling to pay their rent in San Francisco. They noticed that hotels in the area were fully booked during a major conference, prompting them to rent out air mattresses in their apartment. They created a simple website called Airbed & Breakfast to advertise their offer, attracting a few guests and ultimately realizing the potential of their concept. Despite initial skepticism from investors and friends, they pressed on, focusing on building a platform that would allow people to rent their homes to travelers.

Initially, Chesky, Gebbia and fellow co-founder Nathan Blecharczyk faced significant challenges, including the need to gain trust from both hosts and guests in a market dominated by traditional hotels. To tackle this, they listened carefully to their early users, improving their platform based on feedback and introducing features like secure payment methods, verified profiles and reviews. They also took risks by launching marketing campaigns, including an innovative partnership with the Democratic and Republican national conventions to raise awareness.[69]

Airbnb's unique value proposition — offering travelers authentic experiences in local neighborhoods at competitive prices — resonated with consumers. The company saw exponential growth, transforming

---

[69] "Airbnb Commits to Host Over 20,020 Guests for the 2020 DNC and RNC," Airbnb, September 10, 2019, https://news.airbnb.com/airbnb-commits-to-host-over-20020-guests-for-the-2020-dnc-and-rnc/.

from a small startup to a global powerhouse in the hospitality industry. Today, Airbnb operates in more than 220 countries and has millions of listings, demonstrating how a seemingly unconventional idea can lead to monumental success when backed by adaptability and a strong understanding of market needs.

The stories of Blockbuster and Airbnb have a lot to say about the importance of innovation and being attuned to evolving consumer behaviors. Daring to think outside the box, listening to your audience and adapting to feedback can transform a company. Businesses that prioritize adaptability and consumer engagement, truly a market-in approach, are more likely to thrive in an ever-changing landscape.

What is your company's strategy? Does this make a difference for your customers? Do they care? Are you taking risks? If you don't have a differentiated value proposition, you'll never be (or maintain your position as) a market leader. Price alone is not enough; you need to look at what will garnish a premium in the market.

The wall of wins

In 2010, the software company Mailchimp was at a critical juncture. After years of steady growth, it launched a significant product update. The marketing team set an ambitious goal: to increase user engagement by 30% within three months of the launch.

As the deadline approached, the team poured its energy into promoting the new features. They used a combination of email campaigns, social media blitzes and engaging webinars to educate users. After three months, they not only met but exceeded their goal, achieving a remarkable 45% increase in user engagement.

Instead of simply moving on to the next project, Mailchimp CEO Ben Chestnut understood the importance of celebrating this achievement. He organized a company-wide event, inviting every employee from developers to customer service representatives. During the celebration, he presented statistics showing the impact of the team's hard work, including user feedback that highlighted how the new features made a difference in customers' lives.

The event included fun activities, food and a video showcasing testimonials from satisfied users. Chestnut emphasized the importance of each team member's contribution, reinforcing that the success was a collective effort. He even introduced a "wall of wins," a visual display in the office highlighting the team's achievements over the years.

Research shows the power of such celebrations to drive motivation. A study by Socialcast found that 69% of those surveyed would work harder if their efforts were appreciated more.[70]

Following the celebration, Mailchimp experienced a surge in innovation and morale. Employees felt empowered, leading to an influx of new ideas that further improved the company's services. Within a year, user retention rates climbed to 95%, a statistic that significantly contributed to the company's valuation when it was acquired in 2021 for approximately $12 billion.[71]

Mailchimp's experience illustrates that celebrating wins — no matter the size — creates a culture of recognition and motivation, laying the groundwork for future successes.

---

[70] Frayda Leibtag, "The Power of Celebrating Success in the Workplace," *Forbes*, November 14, 2023, https://www.forbes.com/councils/forbescommunicationscouncil/2023/11/14/the-power-of-celebrating-success-in-the-workplace/.

[71] "Behind the Monkey: The Story of Mailchimp's Rise to Email Marketing Dominance," TinySeed, accessed September 17, 2025, https://tinyseed.com/latest/mailchimp-bootstrap-success.

Creating a culture of appreciation

Celebrating even small wins can significantly enhance motivation and engagement. I've found that acknowledging small achievements boosts employee morale and fosters a sense of belonging. By recognizing the efforts of our team, we create a culture of appreciation that drives further success.

Celebrating early wins is especially important because people learn they're going the right way, and you reinforce their direction. Imagine you're hiking and you see the first sign for your trail. It sends you the message that, yes, you're on the right path.

Celebrate first wins and the first change in your team members' mindset. Share stories in the organization about your team's early wins. Make it known that strategy is important. Make heroes out of employees at all levels of the organization who've gone the extra mile. Celebration is an important part of success. The more you celebrate, the more wins you'll have to keep celebrating.

TIFFANY'S TAKEAWAYS

- ◆ **Learn what customers think and feel.** When working on strategy, start with a market-in approach. In your analysis, ask questions like: What's the current state of the market? What's the customer's view of your business, product and/or service? Many companies assume they understand their customers, but few take the time to really learn what customers think and feel.

- ◆ **Take customer feedback to heart.** Expand your data set to include direct customer and non-customer feedback. Once you have the feedback, don't try to justify the answers. Look for what needs to change to be the market leader in your industry.

- ◆ **Dare to think outside the box.** Generate some crazy ideas and start implementing them!

- ◆ **Celebrate milestones.** To keep momentum going, celebrate when your team meets milestones. This gives everyone a chance to pause, reconnect with the mission and receive recognition for a job well done. A celebration could be a lunch, a cake, a town hall event or just a pause in the workday.

Chapter 13

Find Your Next Career Chapter

---

*Retired leaders are in a powerful position
to influence positive change.*

Retirement doesn't have to mean stepping away from leadership — it can be the start of a new kind of impact. Many retired professionals continue to shape their industries and communities through board work, volunteering and mentorship. Serving on a board allows them to lend their experience and wisdom to organizations that benefit from their guidance. Volunteering offers a hands-on way to give back. Mentorship helps prepare the next generation of leaders. With more flexibility and years of insight, retired leaders are in a powerful position to influence positive change, support causes they care about and stay meaningfully engaged.

Becoming a big-picture leader through board work

Ever since I was a child and played "store" for fun, I've loved business. Some people have traditional hobbies — biking, gardening, woodworking, etc.; my hobby is business. It's what I love to do most. If I go to a restaurant, my brain can't shut off. "They could make more money by doing X...." Same thing when I'm shopping at Target; as my eyes wander across the various products,

I contemplate how their arrangement influences consumers' purchasing decisions. I knew that I'd eventually retire from full-time work, but I wanted to keep doing what I love most, so I started exploring the possibility of serving on boards.

Board work is all about helping steer the direction of a company or organization from the top. When you serve on a board of directors, your job is to think big picture — making sure the organization stays on track with its mission, uses its money wisely and has the right leadership in place. It means showing up prepared, asking the right questions and working with other board members to make smart decisions.

Working on a board of directors is different from other leadership roles in a company because it's about governance, not day-to-day management. Unlike executives or managers who are hands-on with operations, board members take a step back to focus on the big picture — strategy, oversight and accountability. Board members ask tough questions, approve major decisions and help guide the company's long-term direction while "staying out of the weeds." It's a challenging leadership role that requires a mix of strategic thinking, independence and trust in the team running the show.

I held my first outside board role when I was CEO of Roche Diagnostics Corporation. It was on a volunteer board at a community hospital. I learned the basics of how to be a good board member and what being on a board was all about. Since then, I've served on a number of private and public boards.

Going into retirement, I knew I wanted to continue doing board work, advising and speaking. I've found board work and board work has found me. Today I'm on three public boards, one private board and two nonprofit boards. Except for one position found through a recruiter, all of my board positions came through people I knew or had worked with.

Considering joining a board?

After a long and successful career as a full-time executive and CEO, my good friend Ann Murtlow knew she didn't want to stop working altogether — but she also didn't want to keep up the same pace. What she really wanted was something more flexible, meaningful and mentally engaging.

"It took me a while to realize it," she said, "but what I really wanted and needed was a portfolio of activities that let me use my experience to add value, learn about businesses I was less familiar with, problem-solve alongside smart and accomplished leaders and have time for all of the parts of life I'd put on hold, like travel, hobbies, old friends and more time with family."

Ann found that balance through board work. Having served on both nonprofit and private company boards for about 20 years, she already knew the territory. When she stepped away from full-time executive roles, she focused on joining public company boards — particularly in sectors she knew well, like utilities, banking and manufacturing.

Interestingly, the parts of board service Ann once liked least are now her favorites. "When I was working full-time, the board role felt like a side gig," she said. "When I briefly stepped away from an executive job, I missed leading people. But now that I'm fully out of the day-to-day marathon, I love being able to focus on strategy and the bigger picture without directly managing teams."

For those considering board work, Ann stresses that it's a serious responsibility. You represent the shareholders. That means being informed, engaged and available — especially when the company faces challenges like mergers, CEO transitions or lawsuits. The work can quickly change from predictable to intense. There are no excuses. You need to be there with your best game.

Ann prepared herself for board work by joining the National Association of Corporate Directors and becoming a Board Leadership Fellow. She also earned board certification and volunteered for a range of committees, gaining experience in audit, compensation, operations, finance and governance.

Her advice for getting started? "Networking is your best friend. Let people know what you're looking for and be specific," she said. "Your best advocates will be those who are well connected and have firsthand knowledge of the value you're capable of bringing.

Board work can have unexpected benefits, including credibility, income, reputation and seeing the other side. Being on a board lets you view the company in a different role than you would in management.[72]

If you're looking to join your first board or increase the number of boards you serve on, networking is essential and important. Keep up your contacts and let people know what you're looking for. Develop an elevator speech, a 60-second overview of where you add value, the role you're seeking and a suggested next step. Understand the special value you can bring to a board. It may be that you're financially competent, tech savvy or strategic.

If you're just getting started, it can be easier to find a seat on the board of a nonprofit organization, which can provide you with a lot of board experience. To find a nonprofit, research what you're passionate about in your community — boards of the American Cancer Society, United Way or arts organizations. Then volunteer and get to know the organization. Let people know you want to be part of their board and help them reach their goals.

---

[72] Future Directors, "Inside the Boardroom," accessed April 30, 2025, https://www.futuredirectors.com/insights/the-4-unexpected-benefits-of-being-on-a-board.

If you're a member of more than one board, consider your board portfolio. Choose industries you want to work in, avoid conflicts that could arise and make sure you can make time commitments.

The Corporate Governance Institute provides training that can help you stay abreast of key policies that can govern how companies need to operate. This knowledge boosts your current career as it broadens your skill base and understanding of business.[73]

As he steps into the next chapter of his career, my friend and colleague Rod Cotton, a former healthcare executive, is focused on doing work that aligns with his personal passions. "At this point, I want to spend my time where I can make a difference," he said. "My board service is about using what I've learned to support missions I really care about, mainly improving access to healthcare and promoting equity, especially for underserved communities." After decades in biotech, pharma and diagnostics, Rod is particularly drawn to efforts around chronic diseases like Alzheimer's and cancer, which have had an impact on his family.

Board service had been on Rod's radar since he was in his early 50s, and back then, he was told board roles typically went to CEOs, chief financial officers or general counsels — not commercial leaders like him. But a few of Rod's mentors encouraged him to take a strategic approach. He started by joining the board of United Way of Central Indiana (UWCI), a $100 million nonprofit.

Rod told me he said "yes" to the United Way not really knowing what it was all about, but feeling like it was the right direction. He believed in the United Way's work as a convener of resources for people in underserved

---

[73] Dan Byrne, "Joining a Board Is a Great Career Move," Corporate Governance Institute, accessed April 30, 2025, https://www.thecorporategovernanceinstitute.com/insights/guides/why-joining-a-board-is-a-brilliant-career-move/?srsltid=AfmBOor2va5sSjpGK-ma31dNwt-EWXv2P2_gf_4CMynquHcbkXmHkjBV.

communities, and he thought that by serving on the board he could be more impactful.

"The UWCI board was a great way to learn about board governance and structure, committee work and how to comport myself," said Rod, who served on the UWCI board for 12 years on key committees like governance, strategy and CEO search. His experiences helped him serve his community. They also served him well in his career and helped him reach his goal to serve on corporate boards.

Now Rod contributes strategic guidance on several boards and advisory panels. He has served or serves as a board member for Community Health Network, Orchard Software (recently sold to Clinisys), Castle Biosciences, Eisai U.S. pharmaceuticals, and more, along with venture partner duties at 2Flo Ventures.

"I know from my own experience serving on boards that simply having a seat at the table can make a huge difference," Rod said. "The perspective I'm able to add as a senior executive — and as an African American — is powerful. I care deeply about issues like fair representation, health equity and including more Black people in clinical trials. When I speak up as a board member, my words have more impact because of my audience and my experience."

What Rod enjoys most about board work is being able to step back and think strategically. "I like working through complex problems and helping companies grow, especially in areas like health tech and innovation," he said. Rod also enjoys connecting with smart, mission-driven colleagues and continuing to learn from other industries.

Rod's advice for leaders exploring board work: Start by figuring out your value. "You need a strong reputation, solid leadership experience and a clear sense of why you want to serve," he explained. Rod recommends formal board education, coaching and lots of networking. "Make sure people know you're interested and ready."

Questions for evaluating board service

When I'm considering joining a new board, I ask myself these questions:

1. **How can I add value?** Having spent my career in healthcare, I tend to join boards where there's a product or service with a patient impact. Instead of thinking, "How do I get on a board?" ask yourself what you can give. Knowing your value and your elevator speech is very important.

2. **What's the company culture?** Being on a board is a team sport, and you want to work with a team that's aligned with your values and sensibilities. How do you do that? During the interview process, go out to lunch with the interviewers. My mom always taught me that the way someone treats servers says a lot about them. While you're at lunch, pay attention. I look out for signs of kindness, compassion and respect.

    These are the qualities a person needs to collaborate well with others. As a matter of fact, while I was out to lunch with one board, the interviewers were rude to the server and I ended up declining the offer.

3. **Do they listen?** There are going to be tough times in an organization, and it's important to be able to challenge existing board members with respect and have honest, open conversations. It's not about everybody agreeing and having the same opinion — that's a whole different problem. It's about being able to really hear diverse opinions and then come to the best decisions based on that listening.

4. **Can I learn?** I'm a lifelong learner, so I want to both contribute and discover. I learn by listening, which is essential in the boardroom and everywhere else.

A legacy of continued leadership

Since retiring from my full-time job, I find joy in serving on boards. I can use my skills in a different way than when I was operationally leading a company. I get an opportunity to work with people outside of my industry who I would never get a chance to work with if I wasn't on a board. Board service provides an educational experience, too, because I'm learning how other leaders approach and solve challenges.

Board service makes me a better leader, too.

Building a legacy doesn't end if you leave your job. Board work offers an opportunity to redefine leadership and legacy in ways that extend far beyond your past positions. There also are powerful avenues to share expertise and encourage others through consulting, volunteering and mentoring. You can find ways to continue to demonstrate value while evolving your leadership. You can leave a legacy that reflects not only professional achievements but also the wisdom and values you've accumulated over a lifetime.

The power of mentorship

Every day, I'm reminded of how powerful mentorship can be. I often mentor people in person and I have regular meetings with individuals I've encountered throughout my career. I don't need a formal title to make an impact; I can share my insights, support others and inspire growth. So can you.

Mentoring isn't about having all of the answers. It's about asking the right questions and inspiring people to really think about their next steps. Where do they want to explore? What do they want to work on? What are their challenges? What paths do they want to take or avoid?

I've learned that mentoring can only happen when both people feel safe enough to speak openly and confidentially about what's really going on. When I'm in a mentoring role, I need to feel comfortable and confident about showing empathy, listening without judgment and building trust. That's important, because mentees can feel vulnerable.

Once, I mentored a leader who had received feedback that she was too polished and distant. This feedback was hard for her to hear, as she felt she had already showed her authentic self. We worked on the issue for months and she experimented with new approaches. For example, she dropped the scripted approach and tried an open Q&A format — which really forces you to think on your feet — and shared a personal story. It was scary in the beginning, but she got good feedback right away and continued to grow. Ultimately, she felt more respected, and her team felt more motivated and connected. Oh, and she got promoted, too.

Seeking mentors of your own can benefit you in unexpected ways, especially if you listen well and keep an open mind. Once, when I was starting a new job, a mentor surprised me by asking, "Who else can carry your torch?" In other words: Who else can bring your strategy through the organization? Who else can help you tell the story? That question really made me stop and think. I realized, if I don't know who those people are, I need to develop them, and we need to make sure we're all aligned so we can move the organization forward.

Giving back is a two-way street. Each time I share a tip or resource, I find fulfillment in watching others thrive. I'm not just imparting knowledge; I'm actively participating in people's journeys and that realization enriches my own life.

We exchange stories, strategies and aspirations and it becomes clear: We're all on this journey of growth together.

Each of us should have many mentors and different mentors at different stages of our careers. What's right one year might not be right the next. Situations and problems change. Over the years I've had many mentors — men, women, young, old, in my industry and outside of my industry. Look for fresh perspectives. When you have a variety of mentors from different backgrounds, you'll have your own personal board of directors.

TIFFANY'S TAKEAWAYS

- **Continue building your legacy.** Serving on a board offers a broader perspective on leadership and is an excellent opportunity to develop new skills and learn from others. If you'd like to pursue board service, take these steps:

  - **Know the rules.** If you're interested in joining a board, first check whether your current employer permits board involvement, as the rules may differ between volunteer and paid boards.
  - **Create a board-specific resume.** Create a resume highlighting the singular value you bring as a board member. A board service resume will be different from a traditional resume. An executive resume highlights specific duties, oversight and quantifiable accomplishments, and a board document presents your career history in a way that emphasizes your leadership skills, including your competency relative to guiding and advising a company.[74]
  - **Let people know you're interested.** Inform your network about your board aspirations. You don't have to make it complicated, just start the journey!

---

[74] Mary Elizabeth Bradford, "Why You Need A Board (Document) Résumé," *Forbes*, October 18, 2023, https://www.forbes.com/councils/forbescoachescouncil/2023/10/18/why-you-need-a-board-document-rsum/.

- ◆ **Create a personal board of directors.** Seek out your own board of mentors and advisors from different backgrounds. Consider guidance from inside and outside your industry. The goal is to surround yourself with people who can give you new angles on how to achieve your goals.

- ◆ **Seek opportunities to mentor others.** Find fulfillment in helping others thrive. When you mentor others, you're not just imparting knowledge; you're actively participating in people's journeys. That realization enriches your own life. Start the mentoring process by asking questions. Mentoring isn't about having all of the answers. It's about inspiring people to think through their next steps.

Conclusion

Your Leadership Legacy

*Step boldly into your future.
You'll shape your legacy with every act of kindness.*

Your legacy is important to me. It's the reason I'm sharing all I know to help you become the leader you want to be.

Regardless of where you are in your career journey, your legacy is about your impact, not your title. It's woven into the connections you make, the laughter you share and the stories you pass down. As you achieve goals and build meaningful relationships, your legacy grows stronger, especially if you hold true to your values.

While you're building your legacy, focus on your priorities. Take time to think about your vision of success. Is what you're doing now what's best for you and your family? Where would you like to be five years from now? If you're not happy with your job or situation, is there something you could change to make things better? Maybe it's time to leave your position and try something new.

It can be scary to take risks, but it's essential. If you never try, you'll never know what you could do or who you could become. What do you have to lose? If the first thing you try doesn't work out, you can always pursue something else.

The road ahead is filled with opportunities to create joy, share wisdom and inspire the people around you. So step boldly into your future. Engage with your community, reach out to colleagues you admire and invest in the next generation. You'll shape your legacy with every act of kindness.

At each stage of your journey, tell your story with confidence. Leadership is about lighting the way for those who follow. It's about lifting each other up. That's why I wrote this book. When I'm mentoring someone or speaking to a group, seeing the spark of curiosity in the eyes of those around me fills me with happiness and a sense of purpose.

My legacy is my gift to you. It's in the content of this book and in my ongoing work to help others — including you — find their way.

I wish you a vibrant and fulfilling life, wherever your journey may take you.

I hope you'll forge a legacy that gives your life meaning and makes an enduring impact.

Featured Leaders

Joe Capper

It was a group interview — which, let's be honest, are the worst. You feel like you're in the hot seat while a bunch of people fire questions at you. But I must've done something right, because they invited me to join. That's how I first met Joe, when a recruiter asked if I'd consider joining his board. Once I learned about the business and got to know Joe, I was all in. He's the real deal — salt of the earth, steady under pressure and the kind of leader who guides teams through tough challenges without ever losing his cool.

Joe's bio

Joe Capper joined MIMEDX in January 2023 to lead the company as chief executive officer and director. A highly experienced and accomplished healthcare executive, he has nearly 30 years of experience in medtech and life sciences leadership roles along with a track record of substantial value creation.

Joe has successfully led several organizations, most recently serving as the CEO of BioTelemetry, guiding the company through a significant turnaround, which culminated with its acquisition by Royal Philips in 2021 for $2.8 billion. Prior to BioTelemetry, he served as president and CEO of both Home Diagnostics and CCS Medical. Joe has a wealth of commercial experience, having held several leadership roles earlier in his career during the decade he spent with Bayer AG. He also was an officer in the U.S. Navy, serving with distinction as a naval aviator.

Joe received his undergraduate degree in accounting from West Chester University in Pennsylvania and a master of business administration degree in international finance from George Washington University in Washington, D.C.

Rod Cotton

Rod and I both worked at Roche Diagnostics Corporation and I always admired him for his strategic mind. He has this amazing ability to see not just where the market is but where it could be — and how to actually get there. My first public speaking gig after I recovered from cancer was for Rod's division. There's this great photo of us from February 2008 — he's holding my hand up in triumph like we've just won something big. For me, it was something big: my health. That photo sits on my desk today.

Rod's bio

Rodney Cotton is a dynamic board member, venture partner and adviser with over 40 years of leadership experience in biotech, diagnostics and tech-driven healthcare. Known for his holistic thinking, bias for action and agile leadership, Rod brings commercial, operational and laboratory expertise to public, private and startup companies.

Rod currently serves as an independent director at Castle Biosciences, sitting on the audit and compensation committees, and is a venture partner at 2Flo Ventures. He also serves on the boards of Eisai U.S., Moleculera Biosciences and Orchard Software and advises General Genomics.

Rod spent over two decades at Roche Diagnostics, where he rose to senior vice president, head of strategy and transformation, and chief of staff to the CEO. At Roche, he led enterprise-wide initiatives, major restructuring and the COVID-19 pandemic response, launching six critical products in 11 months — including the first widely available molecular test. He managed P&Ls exceeding $1 billion and led teams of up to 280.

Rod has been recognized among the most influential corporate directors and most influential black executives by Savoy Magazine and as a top black leader in healthcare by BlackDoctor.org. He received Indiana's Sagamore of the Wabash Award.

He holds a master's in business administration from California State, Dominguez Hills; a master of science in strategic management from the University of Southern California Marshall School of Business; and a bachelor's degree in biological science and sociology from the University of California, Santa Barbara.

Real Leader. Real Legacy.

Cathy Langham

I like to joke that I was Cathy's "house stalker." Cathy and I had the same builder and her home was the model for ours — same layout and everything. She was kind enough to let me come by to check out the space and take photos, even though she was never actually home when I was there. We finally crossed paths at an industry meeting — and from that point on, we've been close. I consider her a dear and trusted friend.

Cathy's bio

Catherine Langham is a seasoned business leader and public board member known for driving business growth, governance, strategic development and team leadership. As founder and CEO of Langham Logistics, Inc., she built a $100 million global transportation and warehousing company offering end-to-end supply chain services across industries including pharmaceuticals and life sciences, food and beverage and automotive.

Cathy holds a bachelor of science degree from Indiana University's Kelley School of Business and received its Distinguished Entrepreneur Award. Her board experience spans diverse sectors — entertainment, retail and grocery — with roles including chairperson of nominating, compensation and governance committees. She has served on the boards of Penske

Entertainment, Celadon Trucking, H.H. Gregg, Inc., The Finish Line, Marsh Supermarkets and the Indiana University Board of Trustees.

Beyond corporate leadership, Cathy has made significant civic contributions. She served as vice chairperson of the 2012 Super Bowl Host Committee, chairperson of the Indianapolis Chamber of Commerce, chairperson of the Central Indiana Corporate Partnership and president of the Indiana Economic Club, supporting regional growth and innovation.

Honors include being named the EY Entrepreneur of the Year, receiving a Sagamore of the Wabash award from both Indiana governors Mitch Daniels and Eric Holcombe and induction into the Indiana Business Hall of Fame as well as being honored as a Living Legend by the Indiana Historical Society. A former member of the Young Presidents Organization, she remains active mentoring future leaders as well as her team. In her downtime, she enjoys golf, biking, travel, reading and family time.

Derek Maetzold

I walked into a Texas saloon — not in cowboy boots, but I did order a whiskey neat. That's when Derek decided I might just fit in. He was looking for a new board member — someone with diagnostic experience, a love for barbecue and a little grit. Lucky for me, I checked all of the boxes and joined the board at Castle Biosciences. What has impressed me most about Derek ever since is his incredible work ethic, genuine care for his team and the kind of steady, thoughtful leadership that earns respect fast.

Derek's bio

Derek Maetzold founded Castle Biosciences in 2007 and initiated operations in late 2008. He is currently president, CEO and a board member of Castle Biosciences. Derek founded Castle Biosciences with the belief that the traditional approach to developing a treatment plan for certain cancers using clinical and pathology factors alone can be improved by incorporating personalized genomic information.

Castle Biosciences represents Derek's first experience in molecular diagnostics. His previous 24 years were spent in pharmaceutical development and commercialization — roughly splitting the time between two multinational pharmaceutical firms and two emerging biotechnology companies. Derek's career in pharmaceuticals was primarily focused on new product development through business development and commercial oversight of pre-approved therapies.

Derek currently serves as a director of PreludeDx, the Coalition for 21st Century Medicine and IMPACT Melanoma. He is also a co-author of numerous publications and a coinventor of multiple technologies.

Derek earned a bachelor of science degree in biology from George Mason University and has done coursework at both The University of Calgary Health Sciences Centre and in the master of business administration program at The University of California, Riverside.

Ann Murtlow

When I stepped into the role of CEO at Roche Diagnostics Corporation, one of my very first visitors was Ann. I figured she was there to talk business — but nope, she came to talk about wild animals! Ann was on the board of the Indianapolis Zoo and was rallying support for the zoo's annual fundraiser, Zoobilation. That was my first glimpse into her big love for animals — and her even bigger heart. Over time, we became great friends and I've had the joy of joining her on plenty of adventures.

Ann's bio

Ann Murtlow began her career as a design engineer at Bechtel, a global engineering, construction and project management company. She later joined AES Corporation, specializing in environmental permitting, and rose to become vice president and group manager, overseeing AES' operations in northern and central Europe. In 2002, she became president and CEO of Indianapolis Power & Light Company (now AES Indiana), where she led a significant organizational turnaround — enhancing the utility's reputation, operational performance and environmental compliance. In recognition of her leadership, she was named Large Utility CEO of the Year in 2010 by "Electric Light & Power" magazine.

In 2013, Ann transitioned to the nonprofit world as president and CEO of United Way of Central Indiana. Over nearly nine years, she restructured the organization's business and impact models, introduced a two-generational approach to combat generational poverty and steered the organization through the COVID-19 pandemic by launching the Central Indiana COVID-19 Community Economic Relief Fund. She retired from this role in June 2022.

An experienced board member, Ann has served in leadership positions on a number of corporate, civic and non-profit boards for more than 20 years. She also served on the board of the Federal Reserve Bank of Chicago for several years during the financial crisis of 2008. Since retiring, Ann has continued contributing her expertise as a board member for organizations including Evergy, Wabash National Corporation and The Mind Trust.

She earned a Bachelor of Science degree in chemical engineering from Lehigh University. Ann's accomplishments have earned her numerous honors, including Indiana's highest civilian honor, the Sagamore of the Wabash in 2022, and the 2020 Torchbearer Award from the Indiana Commission for Women.

About the Author

Tiffany Olson currently serves as a board member for Castle Biosciences, Telix Pharmaceuticals, MIMEDX, Langham Logistics and The Education and Research Foundation for Nuclear Medicine and Molecular Imaging. Past boards on which she's served include Asuragen, BioTelemetry Inc. (a Philips company), ThermoGenesis, Little Rapids Corporation and Diaceutics. Tiffany is a thought leader, speaker and advisor with a goal of inspiring companies to bring their teams to the next level of connection and leadership.

She is a partner at Trusted Health Advisors, consulting on innovative diagnostics. Tiffany retired as president of Cardinal Health Nuclear & Precision Health Solutions, which specializes in radiopharmaceuticals. Prior to Cardinal Health, Tiffany was president of NaviMed, a personalized medicine company. She also worked for Eli Lilly and Company, where she led the strategy to create and commercialize companion diagnostics.

Tiffany worked for Roche Diagnostics for many years, where she attained the position of president and CEO of Roche Diagnostics Corporation. Prior to this appointment, Tiffany was the global head of market development for Roche, located in Basel, Switzerland. Other positions she held in the company included vice president of molecular diagnostics and vice president of corporate accounts. She also spent several years in leading positions with other healthcare organizations.

She was recognized as one of the 10 Best Women Leaders of 2020 by IndustryEra magazine. She was the first woman to receive the Life Science Alley Luminary Award. Tiffany also received the Women of Wellness Award and the American Cancer Society Leadership Award for her volunteer work in oncology. She is an author, blogger, speaker and podcaster on leadership, revenue growth and business strategy.

Tiffany earned a bachelor's degree in business from the University of Minnesota in Minneapolis and a master's degree in business administration from the University of St. Thomas in St. Paul, Minnesota.

The mother of two grown children, Tiffany resides in Indiana with her husband, Brad, and their two Labrador retrievers.

What's Next?

You've reached the end of this book, but your leadership journey is just beginning. The principles you've absorbed and the strategies you've considered are all building blocks of the leader you're becoming.

Real leadership is a practice you refine every single day. The truth is, exceptional leaders are made through continuous learning, honest self-reflection and the courage to keep showing up authentically, especially when it's difficult. They understand that leadership legacy isn't built in a single moment of triumph, but through countless small acts of integrity, compassion and strength.

You have everything you need to lead from exactly where you are. But you don't have to do it alone.

Continue Your Journey

Your investment in yourself and your leadership doesn't end here. At TiffanyOlson.net, you'll find additional resources, tools and inspiring newsletters designed to support you as you continue building your leadership legacy. Whether you're navigating a specific challenge, preparing for your next career move or simply committed to growing as a leader, you'll find practical guidance rooted in real-world experience.

Connect with me on LinkedIn at Linkedin.com/In/OlsonTiffany to join a community of leaders who understand that growth is a lifelong commitment. Share your wins, your questions and your insights. Learn from others who are walking this path alongside you.

Your leadership legacy starts with your next decision. Make it count.

The world needs real leaders — leaders who lead with authenticity, strength and compassion. Leaders exactly like you.

Tiffany Olson

www.ingramcontent.com/pod-product-compliance
Lightning Source LLC
Chambersburg PA
CBHW060502030426
42337CB00015B/1699